ESTATE PLANNING FOR

THE SANDWICH GENERATION:

HOW TO HELP YOUR PARENTS

&

PROTECT YOUR KIDS

CATHERINE HODDER, ESQ.

To my father, Warren, whose wisdom I still treasure.

To my mother, Mary, whose example I try to emulate.

TABLE OF CONTENTS

WHAT TO DO...

INTRODUCTION

Are you a member of the "Sandwich Generation"? That is, do you take care of your children while also caring for elderly parents? According to a recent Pew Research Study: "Nearly half (47%) of adults in their 40s and 50s have a parent age 65 or older and are either raising a young child or financially supporting a grown child (age 18 or older). And about one-in-seven middle-aged adults (15%) is providing financial support to both an aging parent and a child."[i]

Today there are tens of millions of Americans who are part of the Sandwich Generation, and these numbers are escalating as life expectancies increase.

Even if you aren't physically caring for your parents, you may find yourself helping them more often. At the very least, you may be starting to worry about them as they age. If you are reading this book, then you already know in your heart that, in a large part, you are going to be responsible for them in their later years.

What about your children? Do you have protections set up for them such as an insurance policy or designated guardians if something happened to you? What if something happened to them? What if your child is over 18 and became injured in another state? Could you get access to his or her medical information?

You may have some assets, savings, or even a small business. What happens to these when you die? You know you should be making a will and probably need to prepare some other estate planning documents, but which ones? Where do you start?

If have questions about estate planning and how it helps your family, this book is for you.

MISSION

The mission of this book is to guide you through the estate planning process. It will help you begin conversations with your family, and to answer fundamental questions on how to protect your loved ones for what may lie ahead. Each family is unique, and one book cannot deal with every situation. This book is a starting point to get you to think of the future and become better educated about estate planning. It will prepare you to meet with an attorney, banker, or healthcare professional.

General Creighton Abrams is attributed to the quote, "When eating an elephant, take one bite at a time." I think estate planning is like eating an elephant. It can be unbelievably intimidating. How can one plan for their entire future? It is probably one of the biggest reasons people don't get around to it - unless faced with an emergency such as a death or hospitalization of a family member.

Approach estate planning as you would approach the elephant. Take one bite at a time! Have many conversations with your family and follow the steps to organize your information and get the documents you need.

You don't have to do it all at once – you can take your time. And anything you do now is not necessarily set in stone for the rest of your life. You can update these documents as your circumstances change.

This book is designed to walk you through ten easy steps to protect your family, including what documents to have and what to consider. Once you organize your documents, I will provide the foundation for five essential talks to have with your parents and tips on how to handle the challenges of aging parents.

Along the way, there are sidebars with helpful stories or tips. Whenever possible, I will break down the "legalese" (legal terminology) found in many other estate planning books.

It is my goal to give you information to empower you to make the right choices for your family.

ON A PERSONAL NOTE

I started my practice of law in banking and corporate law, later becoming president and general counsel of a finance company. I drafted agreements to protect the company's assets and plan for circumstances if there was a breach of contract.

Although I knew a lot about money and contracts, it wasn't until I had the first-hand experience of caring for my father that I understood the importance of having proper estate planning documents. The more I learned, the more I realized that there is a great deal of information that most people (even attorneys) don't know.

My father was extremely organized. He mentioned to me from time to time about how to handle his affairs when he died. He also made it clear on many occasions that he did not want any artificial means to keep him alive. Knowing full well my mother would not be happy with his decision, I asked him to meet with a lawyer and get that in writing. I told him if there was a dire situation, I would not want to be arguing with my mother about his wishes.

As a result, he consulted with a seasoned estate planning attorney. Our family became grateful for the documents the attorney prepared. Several years later, my father began what became a 10-year battle with Alzheimer's disease. We used each document throughout his long illness and death.

It was because of his durable power of attorney I could access his bank accounts and help my mother pay taxes, make deposits, and pay bills. It was because of his health care power of attorney I could talk to doctors, get medical information, and apply for health benefits for him even though I lived in a different state.

It was because of his advance medical directive that we did not have to debate and decide what measures to take when he was hospitalized. It was because of his last will and testament and his revocable trust that we did not have a long, drawn-out probate and the enormous legal expenses that go along with it. Because of those documents, the financial, healthcare, and probate matters were handled seamlessly. It allowed us to focus on our father's care.

When I went into private law practice in Florida, my partner and I focused on estate planning and business planning. We especially reached out to those families in the "Sandwich Generation" who had young children they wanted to protect and who had real concerns about their aging parents.

We spoke to moms' clubs, church groups, and organizations to spread the word about the importance of estate planning and how key documents can help manage future life events. We made it our mission to educate as many people as possible on estate planning to avoid unnecessary hassles and stress.

It is my sincere hope that in reading this book, you can look at your family's situation and determine what actions you need to take to prepare for challenging times ahead.

DON'T "DO IT YOURSELF"

With all the online legal forms available today, it is tempting to "do it yourself" to save time and money. Short-term savings may cost you more in the long run. Any problems with a last will and testament or a power of attorney are expensive to litigate and can drag out indefinitely.

In their evaluation of three online legal services, Consumer Reports found, "…none of the will-writing products is likely to entirely meet your needs. And in some cases, the other documents aren't specific enough or contain language that could lead to 'an unintended result'."[ii]

Furthermore, most online will services or boilerplate legal forms are not crafted for your exact situation or tailored to your family's needs. No person reviews the documents you create to confirm they are valid and in accordance with your wishes. No company takes responsibility for verifying your will is properly witnessed and notarized according to the laws of your state.

Imagine if your mother named you as the person to handle her medical decisions but the online health care power of attorney form you used was not correct for your state, or you did not have the proper witnesses. The doctors and medical facilities would not be obligated to honor the health care power of attorney.

As the financial power of attorney for your father, imagine if he was hospitalized and you needed to transfer money from one of your parents' accounts to cover taxes or overdrafts.

However, the bank refused to honor the document because it didn't have the proper exculpatory or "hold harmless" language. In this case, the bank is looking for specific language in your document stating they will not be legally liable if they follow those instructions. Banks do not like to be sued, and they will err on the side of inconveniencing you. If the bank doesn't see the proper language, they will refuse to follow the power of attorney document.

The rules and requirements for valid estate planning documents vary from state to state. It is a good idea to use an attorney who is fluent in the ever-changing requirements of your state.

Generally, all the basic estate planning documents (without trusts) from an attorney can range from $400 to $1,500, slightly more with a trust. It is well worth the investment now to avoid potential roadblocks and hassles later. These estate planning documents will be used throughout your life to handle future life events. In an emergency, you don't want to deal with the more difficult issues of enforcement.

In most situations, your loved ones will be the ones dealing with any consequences, expenses, and hardships that result. If there is a mistake with your "do it yourself" or boilerplate document, your family will be the ones paying the attorney fees to fix problems you left behind. You wouldn't want your family to have difficulties over invalid documents during their time of grief. Any investment made now will benefit your loved ones in the future.

➔ **SIDEBAR.** *For people who can't afford a lawyer, some legal aid clinics provide pro bono estate planning services. Search online for legal aid clinics in your community. Additionally, Wills for Heroes is a non-profit service that provides free estate planning services and documents to First Responders. Contact* **www.willsforheroes.com** *for more information.*

PART

ONE

10 STEPS TO CREATE YOUR ESTATE PLAN

Before you go charging into your parents' financial and healthcare decisions, it is wise to educate yourself about estate planning. It doesn't mean you know all the answers, but you should be familiar with the questions asked.

This book will help you to go through your own decisions regarding your financial and healthcare plans. If you don't have any plans or documents, don't worry. Follow the ten steps to put your plan together.

As you complete each step, you will get a firm understanding of the many issues you must contemplate when planning for future life events. Each step will not only prompt you to address specific protections for your children but will also help you identify certain areas your parents may need to consider.

The basic elements of a good estate plan are:

- o Medical Power of Attorney
- o Living Will (Advance Medical Directive)
- o Financial Power of Attorney
- o Last Will and Testament
- o Revocable or Irrevocable Trust (depending on your circumstances)

Depending on where you live, the names of these documents may be different. Some states combine your medical power of attorney with your living will. In California, for example, there is a single document, called an "advance health care directive", that addresses who you want to make your medical decisions (medical power of attorney) and how you want medical treatment administered (living will). In Florida, however, you would have two separate documents, a health care surrogate and a living will. An attorney will know which documents are required by your state.

In addition to getting your estate planning documents together, there are other things to do. Check the titles and beneficiaries of all your property and financial accounts, determine life insurance needs, plan for business succession or termination (if you have a business), and make an "In Case of Emergency" binder.

> *The main reason for putting together your estate plan is to protect your family.*
>
> *The second reason is to open a conversation with your parents.*

You will have much more credibility speaking with your parents about important issues if you have addressed them yourself. For example, if you have figured out your financial power of attorney, you can have an informed discussion on who they want to handle their financial affairs. If you have made your advance medical directives, you can speak from experience when asking your parents about their "end-of-life" wishes.

In the coming chapters, I will walk you through the actions and documents to help you put together your estate plan.

STEP 1

CHECK BENEFICIARY DESIGNATIONS AND PROPERTY TITLES

*"Organizing is what you do before you do something,
so that when you do it, it is not all mixed up."*
– A.A. Milne

You have stuff: money, personal possessions, and property. You might also receive benefits or anticipate benefits from a 401k, retirement accounts, or a pension.

The easiest place to start with your estate plan is to make sure all your beneficiary designations and property titles have the correct names. Beneficiaries are people you name to receive your property once you die.

> **Beneficiary** – One who receives property or a gift from a decedent
>
> **Decedent** – The person who died

Having correct designations is crucial. Why? Because a good deal of your assets can avoid probate (a costly and time-consuming process) and go directly to your heirs.

A probate court determines ownership of assets that don't have a named beneficiary. For example, if you have a bank account in your name only and die, the bank does not know who inherits that account. The bank account becomes part of your estate to be administered during probate. The probate court determines who will receive the proceeds in the bank account by following your last will and testament (if you have one) or by state law if you don't have a will. If, however, you put your spouse or adult child's name as the beneficiary of that account, that bank account would go to them directly without having to go through probate court.

➔ **SIDEBAR.** *You may hear many financial planners and lawyers advise to avoid probate.* **Probate** *is a court proceeding that validates a will and oversees the administration of a decedent's estate. Probate is a lengthy process if you don't have a will. If you do have a will, it is often shorter, but it can still be a time-consuming process. It depends on the jurisdiction. Here is a summary of probate administration:*

- *When someone dies, the executor files the last will and testament with the probate court.*
- *The probate court appoints the executor to act.*
- *The executor collects all the assets of the decedent and alerts creditors of the death.*
- *The creditors have a period when they can file claims against the decedent's estate.*
- *The executor pays claims, outstanding bills, and funeral expenses.*
- *The executor files tax forms on the decedent's estate.*
- *The executor distributes the remaining assets to the heirs.*
- *The executor files a final accounting with the court.*
- *The executor gets a discharge from the probate court.*

All in all, this process can take 18-24 months and sometimes longer. Delays and costs can be significantly reduced if the decedent's property has the proper beneficiary designations.

Executor – One who administers an estate and carries out the wishes in your will, also called a Personal Representative

BENEFICIARY DESIGNATIONS

When you set up bank accounts, investment accounts, or retirement accounts, you name beneficiaries who will inherit these accounts when you die. Called **Transfer on Death** ("TOD") accounts, these operate independently of any instructions to your will.

Say, for example, you set up a savings account when you were 18 and named your mother as the beneficiary. Later you get married but you forget to change your TOD beneficiary designation on that account. You create a will which instructs that all your assets go to your spouse. When you die, the bank does not follow the terms of your will. Instead, the bank honors the TOD designation you made. Therefore, the money in that savings account goes to your mother, who may have predeceased you. If your mother has predeceased you, the account goes to her heirs. The money does not transfer to your spouse.

Check and double-check all beneficiary designations on your financial accounts to make sure they are correct. If you have any life insurance policies, bank accounts, investment accounts, pensions, 401(k) or retirement accounts, check the initial beneficiaries and any alternate beneficiaries. Especially if you have had a significant life event such as marriage, divorce, birth or adoption in your family, you might have some changes. I am willing to bet if you did a careful review of all your beneficiary designations, you will be surprised to find one or more corrections that you need to make.

Do not assume that your bank or financial institution manages your beneficiary designations. For example, if your bank promotes an attractive CD rate and you sign up for a 2-year CD, the bank may not ask for a beneficiary. Even though you might have other accounts at that bank with correct beneficiary designees, the bank may not automatically use your named designee as the one for the new CD account.

→ **SIDEBAR.** *Checking the titling of your property and accounts and confirming your beneficiary designations is an excellent way to protect your family's assets. It also avoids embarrassment. I had a client with a small money market account. At the time he opened the account, he put his longtime girlfriend as the beneficiary and then forgot he did so. Fast forward to ten years later, he is now married to another woman. Upon review of the husband and wife's accounts, his wife discovered that the money market account would have gone to the ex-girlfriend. Awkward! Although it was a nominal amount, changing the beneficiary designation to the wife avoided potentially sticky or embarrassing issues.*

SAFE DEPOSIT BOX

If you have a safe deposit box in your name only, a bank will seal the safe deposit box when you die. Even if a family member has a key, they will not have access to it unless the family member is the personal representative of your estate. It is a good idea to name someone to have access to your safe deposit box.

TITLES ON PROPERTY

In addition to your bank accounts, check titles on the property you own. Review the titles for your cars, RVs, and boats. Often, both spouses have their names on a title. However, a husband may have purchased a vehicle without the wife present, so his name alone is on the title.

Some states make it easy for you to name a beneficiary for your car and have a transfer on death section on the registration document for you to do so. It is easier to retitle documents when the owner is living. Some states have more burdensome requirements to transfer vehicles from a decedent.

TITLES ON REAL ESTATE

Regarding real property, meaning real estate, you have a few options to title the property. The way you title your real property is significant because you can avoid probate and easily transfer ownership to your heirs. These are the most common ways to title real estate:

JOINT TENANCY WITH RIGHT OF SURVIVORSHIP

Joint tenancy with right of survivorship is where two or more owners own property together, all owners' names are on the deed, and each owner has an undivided interest (ownership) in the whole property. Upon the death of one of the owners, their interest automatically transfers to the surviving owners without the need for probate.

TENANCY IN THE ENTIRETY

Tenancy in the entirety is similar to joint tenancy ownership but is reserved for married couples only. When one spouse dies under tenancy in the entirety, the property is transferred automatically to the surviving spouse without going through probate.

TENANTS IN COMMON

Tenants in common is where two or more individuals each own a specific percentage of a property. There is no right to survivorship with tenants in common so an owner can give away or sell their particular interest in the property. Unmarried couples or several people with a common interest in one property may hold property as tenants in common. To illustrate, let's say an unmarried couple purchase a property together. They are tenants in common, each owning 50% of the property. If one of the owners dies, their 50% share (unless stipulated in their will) goes to their heirs, not automatically to the surviving owner.

Check the deeds on your property and determine if they are correct and follow your wishes. If you have a living or revocable trust, which is a good idea if you have real estate, title the property under the trust name. Real estate placed in a trust cuts down on probate expenses and lawyers' fees. There will be more about trusts later.

To summarize, if you title your property correctly and have the proper beneficiaries on your bank, investment, and retirement accounts, you have cut down the confusion of who receives your property and money. These assets will not be caught up in probate court and will be given to your beneficiaries without delay.

STEP 2

REVIEW YOUR INSURANCE NEEDS

*"Fun is like life insurance, the older you get,
the more it costs."*
– Kin Hubbard

According to financial guru Suze Orman, "If a child, a spouse, a life partner, or a parent depends on you or your income, you need life insurance."[iii] This is especially true for those in the Sandwich Generation who may have several dependents.

Life insurance is a tool for income replacement when you die. Its purpose is to cover the costs of paying off a mortgage, funding college for children, and/or providing care for your dependents. Consider disability insurance for income replacement in the event of a long-term disability. Evaluate long-term care insurance for future long-term health care needs.

LIFE INSURANCE

Life insurance should be your first consideration. If you or your spouse died prematurely, how much money does your family require? Do you want money to pay off your house?

Do you need money for your children's education? How much money is necessary to maintain your family's current lifestyle? To determine what coverage is appropriate for your family, you can make a financial needs assessment. A financial needs assessment takes into account your income, expenses, assets, and liabilities, as well as any anticipated benefits and expenses. You can consult a financial planner to help you with this. There are also many online websites with financial needs analysis calculators.

There are two types of life insurance: term and permanent.

TERM LIFE INSURANCE

Term life insurance is designed to provide a death benefit for a designated term of years. Most term policies are for 10, 12, 20 or 30 years. Some families get term policies to cover living expenses and/or college costs in case the primary wage earner dies.

You can think of term insurance as "renting" your insurance, much as you might rent an apartment or an office. You pay a monthly, quarterly, or annual premium (rent) to the insurance company (landlord), and you get a death benefit (roof over your head) until you stop paying. At the end of the term, the insurance company cancels your policy (evicts you). You do not build cash value in your term policy the same way you do not build equity in a property you rent. You do not have any benefits once the policy terminates.

For families who simply want to protect their children until they are financially independent, term life insurance is a good option to consider.

PERMANENT LIFE INSURANCE

Whole life, universal life, and variable life are all examples of **permanent life insurance**, designed to last until you die. If you expect to live until a "ripe old age," and you want to guarantee your life insurance lasts your entire lifetime, consider permanent life insurance. Permanent insurance policies are also designed to build cash value, much like a home builds equity. The premiums (the cost you pay) are more like mortgage payments. They are higher in cost than term premiums, but like mortgages, permanent life insurance can be "paid up," like one can pay off a mortgage. Eventually, you can stop making payments and your coverage still remains in effect.

Each type of permanent life insurance has its own unique features, with too many facets to be described here. When comparing different permanent life insurance policies, verify that any policy you consider has a guaranteed premium, for a guaranteed number of years, and a guaranteed death benefit for life.

One upside of a permanent life insurance policy is that once the policy is in place, it can't be cancelled even if you develop a serious medical condition. The only reasons an insurance company can cancel a life insurance policy is due to nonpayment or fraud (for example, you lied on the application). If you are young and healthy when you get your insurance, you can lock in a much lower premium. Some policies may also let you borrow on your life insurance.

Although permanent life insurance is costlier than term life insurance, it will guarantee that your heirs have money to cover certain expenses. Anyone who has a short-term need for insurance should consider term life because it is the least expensive.

> → **SIDEBAR.** *If you are married but one spouse brings in most of the income, it is tempting to only get an insurance policy on the "breadwinner." Consider a smaller policy or a term policy to cover the stay-at-home spouse. If something happened to him or her, you would need additional funds to pay for childcare, transportation costs to and from activities, meal preparations, laundry and cleaning services, etc. It may be a wise investment to get a cheaper term policy on a stay-at-home spouse until the children are out of the nest.*

To obtain a life insurance policy, most insurance companies will want some medical information or even lab work for insurance. The amount of coverage requested determines the medical requirements.

An insurance agent can guide you about how much life insurance is best for your situation. The goal is to replace your income so your family can survive without you. You do not have to leave your dependents with a huge windfall or more money than they can handle.

DISABILITY INSURANCE

Disability insurance may also benefit your family's situation. Disability insurance covers a working individual in the event where they may not be able to continue working due to an accident or severe illness. While the probability of this happening may seem remote, according to the Social Security Administration, a 20-year-old worker has a 1-in-4 chance of becoming disabled before reaching full retirement age.[iv]

Social Security provides disability payments for long-term disabilities; those whose illness may last over one year or result in death. A handful of states also provide disability benefits.[v] The process to collect these benefits can be long and the payments may not cover all your family's expenses.

If not provided by your state, disability insurance can be employer paid or purchased individually.

EMPLOYER PAID GROUP DISABILITY INSURANCE

Your employer insures your paycheck if you become ill or injured and can no longer work. There are short-term disability income policies, that generally only pay for three months. There are also long-term disability income policies, that kick in after the short-term disability term ends and pay you until "normal retirement" at age 67.[vi] Because your employer provides this benefit to you, any benefit you might receive would be reported as taxable income.

INDIVIDUAL DISABILITY INCOME INSURANCE

If you are self-employed or your employer does not provide group coverage, you can purchase your own policy. The nature of the work you do, your age, and your income determine the benefits you can buy and the cost of the coverage. The "riskier" your job or the more likely you are to become disabled results in higher premiums. The advantage of a private disability plan is that you can shop around for the best plan and you won't lose coverage if you change jobs or companies.

For highly compensated employees and professionals, group insurance often has limited benefit amounts that would not fully cover their total compensation. In these situations, these highly compensated individuals can purchase supplemental individual disability policies, to insure their total compensation above the limits of their employer's insurance.

➔ **SIDEBAR.** *My friend's brother-in-law is a surgeon. The nature of his work is directly related to his ability to perform surgery. If he injures his hand, his family income would suffer significantly. He says his most important monthly bill is his disability insurance premium.*

Statistically speaking, a person in any age group is more likely to sustain a long-term disability (one lasting 90 days or more) than dying prematurely.[vii] Disability insurance is important for anyone who relies on their income to support their household. Find out if your employer provides disability insurance and talk to a few insurance brokers to see what coverage may be appropriate for your situation. Determine when the disability payments will pay out and if there is a waiting period to receive them. Find out how long the payments will continue. There may be limits on how much a policy pays and what is considered a disability. While you may ultimately decide against a policy, it is a good idea to get the facts and do an analysis for your family's situation.

LONG-TERM CARE INSURANCE

Consider your family's need for **long-term care insurance**. Long-term care insurance is insurance that provides coverage for costs of long-term health care not covered by your health insurance, Medicare, or Medicaid.

Carriers of long-term care policies now provide benefits regardless of where you receive care. This is especially attractive if you wish to stay in your home. You do not need to be in a healthcare facility to receive benefits. Look for coverage that includes the expenses of home care, adult day care, respite care, assisted living facilities, nursing homes, and Alzheimer's care. When evaluating long-term care policies, ask the company what benefits they cover and when the benefits begin.

Generally, long-term care begins upon the loss of two **activities of daily living**: eating, bathing, dressing, toileting, walking, and continence. As with all insurance, age and health determine the cost. The younger you are, the less costly the premiums, and the more likely you are to qualify for coverage.

Long-term care insurance policies help pay for the cost of care, so you don't have to worry about running out of money. For the affluent, these policies are designed to preserve assets. Traditional policies offer level premium payments, that is, premium payments that stay the same; but even these may be subject to rate increases. Alternatively, policies are now available that only require a single, one-time payment. These are becoming increasingly popular because they are not subject to rate increases. These also provide a death benefit; if you never use the benefits, your beneficiary receives a death benefit, generally equal to the amount of the one-time payment.

When exploring any type of insurance coverage, talk with an experienced insurance broker who can understand and present the best insurance options for your family. The broker will provide quotes from various insurance companies. Ask your broker about the reputation of the insurance company. Are they solvent? Do they have a good track record of paying claims?

> → **SIDEBAR.** *As your life circumstances change, so will your insurance needs. Find an* **insurance agent** *you are comfortable talking with and who understands your family situation. Finding a reputable insurance agent isn't hard. Get referrals or recommendations from friends or family. Research them on the internet and read any reviews about them. Find out what licenses or certifications they have and their years of experience. All states have insurance departments that regulate insurance companies. Check to see if the company is licensed and if there are any complaints filed against that company.*

Having appropriate insurance is a key component to any estate plan. It is worth doing the research and talking to an insurance professional to see what makes the best sense for your specific situation.

STEP 3

NAME YOUR
HEALTH CARE POWER OF ATTORNEY

"Never go to a doctor whose office plants have died."
– Erma Bombeck

A **Health Care Power of Attorney** is a legal document in which you designate someone you trust to have access to your health information and to make all the decisions relating to your care and comfort in the event of your incapacity. Depending on your state this document could be called a **Health Care Surrogate, Medical Power of Attorney, Health Care Power of Attorney** or **Durable Power of Attorney for Health Care.** Your designee is called a Health Care Surrogate, Health Care Proxy, Health Care Agent, or some other title. So "health care surrogate" can refer to a document or a person. To avoid confusion, I will refer to the document as a "health care power of attorney" and the person as the "health care surrogate."

If you are incapacitated, it means you are unable to make medical decisions for yourself. The incapacity could be short-term such as temporarily losing consciousness in a car accident. Or it could be long-term such as a having a severe stroke or being in a coma.

The health care power of attorney is an important document to get around increased privacy and HIPAA (Health Insurance Portability and Accountability Act) regulations, especially if family members travel or live around the country. Doctors and medical facilities may be reluctant to share information without proper power of attorney documentation.

HOW TO CHOOSE A HEALTH CARE SURROGATE

Choosing a health care surrogate can be difficult. Look for someone that can understand medical information and will follow your instructions. Talk with them regarding your wishes and make sure they are willing and able to honor them. In determining the best choice for your health care surrogate, ask yourself the following questions:

Is your health care surrogate strong and forceful enough to deal with doctors and meddling family members? You don't want your designee to be intimidated by medical personnel or family members who think they know better than what you want.

Do they have common sense? Meaning, can they rule from their head and not their heart? Will they avoid unnecessary or risky surgical procedures? You want them to do everything to keep you alive and in good health. But it may not be in your best interest if they approve a triple-bypass when you are 97 years old and in failing health.

Can your health care surrogate understand medical issues involving your care? Do they take the time to ask questions of doctors or seek second opinions? You don't want your surrogate to blindly follow a doctor's advice or be afraid to ask questions. Do they know to ask about any new medications affecting your current prescribed medications?

Will they know what information is appropriate to share with family members and friends? You want someone who is familiar with your family dynamics and sensitivities. For example, you might want to keep certain conditions private such as being HIV positive or having mental health issues. Your surrogate should know what information to keep confidential.

Do they live close enough to you to be able to visit hospitals or care facilities? It is a burden on your health care surrogate to handle medical issues and personnel remotely. Ideally, your health care surrogate is able to be on location to supervise your care and comfort and is aware of what you need.

WHAT GOES INTO A
HEALTH CARE POWER OF ATTORNEY

Although the language may vary widely in a health care power of attorney document, there are three common provisions: identification and designation, statement of powers and termination.

IDENTIFICATION AND DESIGNATION. You name who is authorized to make your health care decisions if you are unable to do so, meaning you are incapacitated. You may specify that one or more physicians must certify in writing that you are incapacitated for the health care power of attorney document to take effect. Your state may have a specific number of required certifications.

You provide the name and contact information (address, telephone) of your health care surrogate. It is a good idea to have backup designations of alternate surrogates in case your first choice is unavailable or unable to serve.

While you may be tempted to put two people to act as "co-health care surrogates" to spare feelings, say both your son and daughter, it could cause friction and problems if they disagree. Instead, list one health care surrogate and a backup surrogate. You may want to communicate your reasons for choosing your health care surrogate so there is no resentment among family members.

STATEMENTS AND POWERS. Your health care power of attorney document will have a statement that your health care surrogate must comply with any advance medical directive (living will) or directive given by you. It may also include, among other things, the powers to consult with health care providers, make health care decisions, hire or fire medical professionals, apply for public benefits such as Medicare or Medicaid, release medical records and information to others who provide for your care, and transfer or admit you to a healthcare facility.

TERMINATION. The health care power of attorney terminates upon your death or upon the death of your surrogate. That is why it is a good idea to name one or more alternate surrogates. You can always revoke or change your health care surrogate if you wish.

State laws have a strict protocol for proper signatures and witnessing for the health care power of attorney to be valid. It is a good idea to have an attorney draft one for you.

> → **SIDEBAR.** *If you have children who are 18 years or older, consider getting a health care power of attorney on them. If they are away at college, studying abroad, or living in a different town, you may not be able to get access to their medical information or help with medical decisions in the case of an accident or emergency. Due to HIPAA privacy laws, medical professionals are reluctant to divulge or discuss any information without that document. Even if your child can make medical decisions for themselves, you may also want access to their health records and be able to speak with their doctors, especially If you are still paying for their medical care. An alternative to a health care power of attorney is to have your child sign a HIPAA release form <u>for each doctor</u> permitting them to release information about your child to you.*

Make sure you give a copy of your health care power of attorney to your health care surrogate for safe keeping. It is a good idea to let your loved ones know who is responsible for making decisions about your health care.

Do not confuse a health care power of attorney with a living will or advance medical directive. Some states combine a health care power of attorney with an advance medical directive. The next section explains advance medical directives.

STEP 4

MAKE YOUR LIVING WILL (ADVANCE MEDICAL DIRECTIVE)

"I'm not afraid to die, I just don't want to be there when it happens."
– Woody Allen

An **Advance Medical Directive** or **Living Will** is a legal document in which you declare, in the event of a <u>terminal</u> or <u>end-of-life</u> condition, to withhold or withdraw life-prolonging measures.

This document comes into effect if you have an incurable, irreversible illness or disease that will result in death. If you were in that situation: Do you want your body to be sustained with breathing equipment, nutrition, and hydration tubes? Or do you want to die naturally?

It is important to determine what measures you want (or don't want) to artificially extend your life. While this is an unpleasant decision to think about, it is more distressing to your loved ones who may be faced with these decisions, especially if there is a difference of opinion. The advance medical directive takes the burden of those difficult decisions away from your family and avoids disagreements among family members.

Determine if and what "heroic measures" are to be taken to prolong your life when you are terminally ill. You can decide to withhold food (feeding tubes) and water (administration of IV fluids), but still be given medications to be free from pain or discomfort.

Don't confuse advance medical directives with a **"Do Not Resuscitate Order,"** called a "DNR." A DNR is a medical order which states that if your heart stops beating or you stop breathing, doctors will not perform CPR or put you on life support.

→ **SIDEBAR.** *Advance medical directives vary widely from state to state in terms of language and what you may specify. Keep this in mind if you live close to another state and it is possible you might receive healthcare or be admitted to a medical facility in the other state. While your document may still be enforceable, you might face extra challenges. Make sure your document complies with those states where you might receive treatment.*

WHAT GOES INTO AN
ADVANCE MEDICAL DIRECTIVE

An advance medical directive has common statements that inform your doctors, health care surrogate, and family of your wishes.

STATEMENT THAT YOU ARE BOTH MENTALLY AND PHYSICALLY INCAPACITATED. You must be at a point where you do not have the power or ability to speak or make decisions on your behalf.

STATEMENT THAT YOU DO OR DO NOT WANT YOUR DEATH TO BE ARTIFICIALLY PROLONGED. You might indicate under which circumstances you want intervention or lack of intervention such as when you are facing a terminal condition, an end-stage (end-of-life) condition, or in a persistent vegetative state.

STATEMENT BY ONE OR MORE PHYSICIANS. Depending on your jurisdiction, you may need one or more physicians to determine that there is no reasonable medical probability of your recovery from your condition.

STATEMENT REGARDING COMFORT AND PAIN MEDICATION. You can direct that you want to die naturally but allow administration of medication or a medical procedure necessary to provide comfort or care or alleviate pain.

STATEMENT OF YOUR INTENT. You declare that this is your final expression of your legal right to refuse medical or surgical treatment and you accept the consequences of such refusal. This is the ultimate statement that can take away the guilt or stress from your family. The decision is yours alone and no one can second-guess your wishes.

Due to the nature of the document, the advance medical directive has strict witnessing requirements. If you are serious about how you want a terminal condition handled, this is one document not to "do it yourself."

Give a copy of your advance medical directive to your health care surrogate, your doctor, and your loved ones. It is also a good idea to file a copy with your local hospital or medical facility.

→ **SIDEBAR.** *Gaining popularity among hospitals and medical professionals are* **POLST** *(Physician Orders for Life-Sustaining Treatment) forms. A POLST form does not replace your advance medical directive. Instead, it works with it and allows you to give more detailed treatment instructions in a medical emergency. This form is usually made on pink paper to stand out among other medical paperwork. This form should only be used if you have advanced frailty or an end-stage illness. For more information, visit* **www.polst.org**.

STEP 5

NAME YOUR FINANCIAL POWER OF ATTORNEY

"By failing to prepare, you are preparing to fail."
– Benjamin Franklin

A **Durable Power of Attorney**, also called a **Financial Power of Attorney**, is a legal document which allows you to designate an "agent" to make all your financial and business decisions.

> **Agent** – A person you designate to act as your power of attorney, also called "attorney-in-fact"

You can use a durable power of attorney if you are hospitalized, in a coma, or even just out of the country. A durable power of attorney is not contingent on you being unable to handle the transactions yourself. If you have one or more businesses or private accounts, you may want someone stand in for you to manage your affairs if you can't.

A durable power of attorney can also be a document of convenience. It is helpful when one spouse travels frequently and isn't available to sign things. For example, I had a client who has power of attorney for her husband to close real estate deals when he is away on business. Another client gave her daughter power of attorney to pay bills and manage all the finances for her because the client preferred not to handle it herself.

You may also create a durable power of attorney which will only be activated if you are truly incapacitated. This is called a **"springing" power of attorney**, that "springs" into action if you are truly incapable of handling you own affairs. This power of attorney must define the incapacity and specify what will trigger the power of attorney to become active. For example, you can instruct that two physicians must certify that you are unable to make decisions for yourself.

Because a "springing" power of attorney limits when a power of attorney is authorized to act, it can cause delays. If you are incapacitated, it may take some time for your designated agent to find two physicians to sign off on your incapacity. In the case of Alzheimer's disease or dementia, mental incapacity could be gradual. Although you are unable to manage your affairs, a doctor may be uncomfortable making such a definitive claim. Your agent would have to go to court to get a determination of your capacity which defeats the purpose your power of attorney document. An estate planning attorney can discuss the pros and cons with you to guide you to the best power of attorney document for your circumstances.

HOW TO CHOOSE AN AGENT

The individual you designate as your power of attorney is called an "agent" and must be at least 18 years of age and competent to serve. That means they are able to carry out their responsibilities as your agent. It is essential to choose someone you trust implicitly to handle your affairs and someone who can make sound financial decisions for you.

You should designate an agent who is responsible, organized, and understands finances. Your agent should be comfortable talking with bankers, financial advisors, attorneys, and accountants. They must understand the serious commitment they are undertaking.

What if you don't have someone who can act as your power of attorney? For a fee, a bank, lawyer, or accountant will serve as your agent. Some people choose to have a third-party act as their agent for convenience or to avoid family disputes. For example, one husband and wife had their accountant serve as their agent. Since their five adult children were living in all different parts of the country, none living nearby, the couple thought it would be easier for everyone to have a neutral party involved.

Choose your agent wisely. Since they can act on your behalf, your agent can bind you to the decisions they make. Any agent you designate has a fiduciary duty to act in your best interest. If they do otherwise, they may be civilly or criminally liable. For example, your agent may lack the necessary accounting expertise to handle your money and taxes. It would be in your best interest if they hired an accountant. If, however, your agent uses your money to take a cruise, they are self-dealing and not acting in your best interest.

WHAT GOES INTO A
DURABLE POWER OF ATTORNEY AGREEMENT

There are four important elements within a durable power of attorney agreement: identification and designation, list of powers, statement to third parties, and termination.

IDENTIFICATION AND DESIGNATION. A statement that the following individual is designated to make your financial decisions. You name your primary agent and a backup agent if your first choice could not serve.

LIST OF POWERS. This is an enumerated list of what the agent can and cannot do in your place. For example, some powers may be: paying bills and taxes; handling banking and other financial institution transactions; handling investment or real estate transactions; handling any sales of personal property or business transactions; handling insurance premiums and claims; acting in all estate and trust matters; suing on your behalf (for example, if your incapacity was caused by an accident) and handling lawsuits; doing all things to continue the support and maintenance of your family; obtaining governmental, civil, or military benefits for you; and handling your taxes and retirement.

Some powers which you may not want to authorize (or are prohibited to be authorized by state law) include: power to vote in elections, power to make gifts to qualify for public benefits, power to create a revocable trust, power to amend or terminate any trust you created, or the power to change beneficiary designations.

STATEMENT TO THIRD PARTIES. This is a statement that any person or entity (for example, a bank) that relies on this power of attorney will be indemnified or held harmless for transacting matters with your agent. Again, banks or financial institutions do not want to get in trouble if they follow your instructions. It is critical that financial institutions see this clause in your power of attorney document so they cooperate with your agent.

TERMINATION. The durable power of attorney terminates on your death or the death of your agent. That is why it is a good idea to name one or more alternate agents. Your alternate agents should also meet the stringent criteria for trustworthiness and competence as your primary agents. Do not appoint someone you can't trust.

A durable power of attorney is a powerful document, and the legal requirements vary from state to state. It is a good idea to have an attorney draft one for you and discuss the individual powers that are conveyed to your agent.

> ➜ *SIDEBAR. In certain circumstances, consider a "limited" power of attorney. This is a short document which allows you to designate a person to handle a specific transaction for you. For example, you may use a limited power of attorney to have someone transfer a motor vehicle title on your behalf. The power terminates upon a specified time or the conclusion of the transaction.*

If at any time you wish to revoke a power of attorney, you must draft a **Revocation of Power of Attorney**. Give this document to your original agent and any banks, financial institutions, etc. that may have your original power of attorney on file. For this reason, keep a record of who has a copy of your power of attorney.

STEP 6

MAKE YOUR LAST WILL AND TESTAMENT

"Someone is sitting in the shade today because someone planted a tree a long time ago."
– Warren Buffet

Don't have a will yet? You are not alone. According to a 2017 Caring.com poll, 58% of Americans don't have a will.[viii]

Think of a will as an investment in your family's security. If you die **"intestate"**, meaning without a will, a court determines where your property will go and decides who will raise your minor children. While it is unpleasant to think about, if you have children under the age of 18, it is crucial that you have a plan in place to protect your children.

Everyone who dies goes through probate. If you don't have a will, the court follows intestate rules to determine who inherits your estate. Probate administration takes time and costs money in terms of probate fees and attorney expenses. With a will, the process is easier and less expensive. With a will and trust, probate is even more streamlined with minimal expense, but more about trusts later.

Additionally, you may not like the result of the intestate

laws. You may assume that if you are married and your spouse dies without a will, his or her estate will go to you. Not so fast! Under most intestate laws, which vary from state to state, you might receive 1/3 to 1/2 of his or her estate, and the remainder goes to your children.

In California, for example, if you are married with no children, and your spouse died intestate, you do not inherit everything. Instead, you would inherit all of the community property that you own with your spouse and 1/2 of his or her separate property. Separate property is what your spouse acquired before the marriage. The other 1/2 of your spouse's separate property would go to his or her parents. You have much more control of your assets and can avoid unintended consequences if you prepare a will.

WHAT DOES A WILL DO?

A will allows you to name who handles your property and estate (personal representative), who cares for your minor children (guardian), and who inherits your assets and estate (beneficiaries). If you don't decide, a court decides for you and you may not like the result.

In making a will, you must answer three critical questions:

o   Who do you want to take care of your children?

o   Who do you want to handle the distribution or maintenance of your estate?

o   Who do you want to inherit your estate?

WHAT GOES INTO A WILL

A last will and testament can be simple or complex. It can be one page or 100 pages. In some states, you can even handwrite your will without witnesses, called a "**holographic will.**" A holographic will must be written entirely by hand (not typed), and in some states dated. It does not require witnesses to the will. In fact, having a witness does not make it a holographic will. But proving the validity of a handwritten will can be tricky. And there are often errors or ambiguities. A holographic will is subject to probate so any questions or unclear provisions must be litigated which takes time and money.

An attorney can draft a comprehensive last will and testament for your specific circumstances. They make sure your will is valid, complies with witnessing requirements, and avoids ambiguity. With a properly drafted will, the probate process is much more efficient and therefore less costly for your estate.

There are some standard provisions you might see in a will, and it is a good idea to familiarize yourself with these provisions and think about how they would apply in your situation.

PREAMBLE. This is where you see an opening statement such as:

> "*I, **Your Name**, of **Your County**, **Your State**, do hereby make, publish and declare this to be my LAST WILL AND TESTAMENT, and hereby revoke all prior wills and codicils previously made by me.*"

This statement makes sure that this latest will is considered the last and final statement of your wishes. If you made any other wills before, they are not valid and automatically revoked.

IDENTIFICATION. This is where you state if you are married and if you have children. If you are married, you identify your spouse by his or her name and any aliases (other names they might go by). If you have children, you identify them by name here. There will also be a statement such as:

> *"All references in this will to 'my children' are to my child(ren) named above as well as any other children of mine born or adopted after the execution of this will. All references in this will to 'my descendants' are to my children and their descendants."*

So, rest assured, if you were to make your will and later had other children or adopted other children, they will be included even if you didn't have time to update your will to add them by name.

DEBTS AND FUNERAL EXPENSES. This provision directs your personal representative to pay all claims against your estate. This includes legal debts, funeral expenses, legal expenses connected to the administration of your will, as well as any taxes such as estate, inheritance, and transfer and succession taxes.

Under estate and trust law, creditors are paid before money goes to beneficiaries. You can't rack up a bunch of debt and expect that all your money will go to your beneficiaries, leaving your creditors high and dry.

MEMORANDUM OF SPECIFIC BEQUESTS. A **memorandum of specific bequests** ("Memorandum") is a separate writing, signed and dated by you, that lists gifts of tangible personal property (your possessions) to specific beneficiaries.

Some states do not allow a separate writing, so this list will be written in your will.

> **Bequest** – a gift or inheritance given in a last will and testament

Tangible personal property is usually those items that are meaningful to your family and couldn't be equally divided, such as jewelry, china, silverware, antiques, furnishings, books, etc. In the Memorandum, you list the particular item with detail and name the specific beneficiary. For example, you shouldn't write *"my ring to my daughter,"* but instead you should write, *"my diamond engagement ring with three diamonds in a gold setting to my daughter, **Legal Name of Beneficiary**."*

You might also mention in your will that the cost of packing and delivering the items are to be paid from your estate as an expense of administration. Your niece might appreciate your antique tea set more if she didn't have to pay for it to be packed and shipped herself.

The benefit of having a Memorandum as a separate writing is that you can change it without having to rewrite your will. If you have a falling out with a beneficiary, you can easily change these instructions to apply to another beneficiary. You can also add and delete items as you acquire them or dispose of them.

Finally, in the Memorandum section, you state that if no separate writing was found after a reasonable search, your tangible personal property will become part of your estate (called the residuary estate) to be given to the beneficiaries you have named in the will. Therefore, if you did not get around to making a Memorandum, your tangible personal property will go back into your estate for your named beneficiaries.

→ **SIDEBAR.** *Another advantage of the Memorandum is that a writing coming from you is a powerful way to settle family squabbles. Two siblings couldn't argue over the same painting "mom promised them" if mom puts it in writing. Emotions run high after a death in the family. Understanding and accepting mom's wishes is much easier when it is spelled out and helps avoid family fights.*

SPECIFIC BEQUESTS. This provision states that any tangible personal property not mentioned in the memorandum of specific bequests (discussed above) will go to your beneficiaries. For example, you might leave everything to your spouse first, but if your spouse has predeceased you, your tangible personal property will then go to your children or other beneficiaries you name.

This section is where you might mention other specific gifts, such as a car, boat, shares of stock or interest in a business concern. List these bequests with particular details, such as a Vehicle Identification Number (VIN) for a car or a boat. For stock in a business, you might include a statement such as:

*"I give all of my stock (including any dividends, rights and benefits declared at the time of death) which I may own at the time of my death in **Corporate Name of Company** or its successors whether by change of name, consolidation or merger, to **Legal Name of Beneficiary**; provided that if he/she fails to survive me, this gift shall lapse and go into residuary estate."*

Under specific bequests, you can also provide for monetary gifts, gifts of specific property, charitable gifts, and for the guardianship of your pet(s).

MONETARY GIFTS. For a monetary gift, meaning cash, you may include a statement such as:

> *"I give $5,000 to, **Legal Name of Beneficiary;** provided that if he/she fails to survive me, this gift shall lapse and go into residuary estate."*

GIFTS OF SPECIFIC PROPERTY. For gifts of specific items or property, such as a vehicle, RV, or boat, you may include a statement such as:

> *"I give my 1966 Chevrolet Corvette Stingray (VIN#) to, **Legal Name of Beneficiary**; provided that if he/she fails to survive me, this gift shall lapse and go into residuary estate."*

If you are not in possession of the item at the time of your death, the gift is considered taken away, or **adeemed,** meaning the gift is void. Your beneficiary does not receive your specific gift. For example, if you put in your will that your nephew is to receive your '66 Corvette but you sold that Corvette before your death, your nephew does not have any claim on your estate. He does not receive a '66 Corvette nor proceeds from your estate equaling the value of a '66 Corvette.

Finally, consider including a statement that if your beneficiaries are unable to agree upon a method of distribution among themselves, your personal representative will determine the distribution.

CHARITABLE GIFTS. A specific bequest provision is where you can make charitable gifts. You could give a certain sum of money to a favorite charity or you could give a certain percentage of your residuary estate to a charitable institution. For example:

> *"I give $2,000 to Habitat for Humanity."*

> *"I give 10% of my residuary estate to the American Red Cross."*

CARE FOR YOUR PET(S). A specific bequest could also provide for the guardianship and care of your pet(s). Pets are considered property and your will can instruct who inherits your pet along with any monetary provisions for your pet's care. A statement might be:

> *"I give my dog, Charlie, and whatever pets I own at the time of my death to **Legal Name of Beneficiary**. I also give $5,000 to provide for the lifetime care of my pet(s). Should **Legal Name of Beneficiary** predecease me, I give my pet(s) to **Legal Name of Backup Beneficiary** along with the $5,000."*

On a side note, if you had particular wishes on the care of your pet, you might consider writing a letter to the beneficiary of your pet. You can also have an attorney set up a trust for your pet. A **pet trust** allows you to give details about the care for your pet and instructions on what to do if the pet gets sick, dies, etc.

> → **SIDEBAR.** *Be careful when making specific gifts because they get priority over a residuary estate. To illustrate, if you make a specific bequest for $20,000 to be given to your favorite charity but your estate is only worth $10,000 at your time of death, the charity receives $10,000 and your heirs get nothing. If instead you make a bequest giving the charity 10% of your residuary estate, the charity receives $1,000 and your heirs receive $9,000.*

RESIDUARY ESTATE. This is a catchall clause. It gives the rest of your estate, not already given to others, to your named beneficiaries. If it wasn't given away in a prior specific bequest, it goes to your beneficiary or beneficiaries.

Under this clause, you also designate back up beneficiaries. For example, if you leave everything to your spouse but your spouse predeceased you, your will instructs that your estate goes to the other beneficiaries (i.e., your children).

When giving your estate to your children, you must specify whether the bequest is given **per stirpes** or **per capita**. Per Stirpes is a legal term which means "of the branch." Per Capita means "by the head." I have included examples of per stirpes and per capita on the following pages to help illustrate.

AN EXAMPLE OF PER STIRPES

You have three children: Alex, Ben and Charlie.
Alex has two children (your grandchildren) Dave and Dan.
Ben and Charlie do not have children.

You want your three children, Alex, Ben and Charlie, to share equally in your estate. Therefore, each child would inherit 1/3 of your estate.

Alex (1/3)   Ben (1/3)   Charlie (1/3)

However, what if Alex predeceases you? Do you want Ben and Charlie to inherit Alex's 1/3 share? Or do you want Alex's children to inherit the share that would go to Alex? Under Per Stirpes, Alex's 1/3 share of the estate goes to his children, so Dan and Dave would each inherit 1/6 of the overall estate.

TO ILLUSTRATE PER STIRPES

AN EXAMPLE OF PER CAPITA

Under **Per Capita** distribution, it goes by the head. If your living beneficiaries are Alex, Ben, Charlie (your sons) and Dan and Dave (sons of Alex). Each will share equally. Therefore Alex, Ben, Charlie, Dan and Dave will each receive 1/5 of your estate.

TO ILLUSTRATE PER CAPITA

However, if Alex predeceases you, the estate will be divided among the <u>then living beneficiaries</u>. Therefore, Ben, Charlie, Dan, and Dave will each receive 1/4 of your estate.

As you can see, bequests can sometimes get tricky. That is why it is a good idea to consult an attorney who can see several steps ahead and help you avoid unintended consequences.

DISINHERITANCE CLAUSE. This provision allows you to disinherit anyone who otherwise might be entitled to receive your estate. While it is your prerogative to disinherit anyone, think carefully about doing so and your reasons for doing it. State laws protect spousal rights and prohibit you from disinheriting your spouse. If a surviving spouse is left out of the will or specifically disinherited, they may be entitled to opt for an **elective share** of your estate. Depending on the jurisdiction, an elective share might be 1/2 to 1/3 of the decedent's estate.

There are safeguards for minor children as well. Some states have inheritance rights for children to protect them until the age of 18. They would otherwise become wards of the state if no one else can provide for them. You may not disinherit them.

If you intend to disinherit a child or grandchild, it is wise (and sometimes required depending on the jurisdiction) to specifically state that you are disinheriting that person. Otherwise, a court may think you "forgot" which is a protection for children and may open your will to be challenged. It is often a good idea to explain your reasons for doing so to avoid misunderstandings. For example, you might explain that you are disinheriting your son, who you know is successful and thriving, so you may give your entire estate to your daughter who has a life-long disability.

You might be considering "cutting" a beneficiary out of your will due to some issue, such as the child can't handle money responsibly or has problems with addiction. However, there are ways to leave them some money that is managed for them through trusts. I will talk about trusts in the next chapter.

➔ **SIDEBAR.** *Think twice about who you disinherit! I had a wealthy client with three grandchildren, one of whom was not good at keeping in touch with the grandmother. The grandmother wanted to disinherit the inattentive grandchild out of spite or "to show her who's boss." I counseled my client to think about the ramifications in which two grandchildren would inherit but one would not. Will the one grandchild hold ill feelings against her siblings? Will the two siblings be made uncomfortable in accepting the inheritance when their sister was frozen out? How will the grandmother be remembered by all the grandchildren: generous or spiteful? Upon reflection, the grandmother relented and did not disinherit the grandchild. Subsequently, the grandmother repaired her relationship with her prodigal grandchild. I'm glad she reconsidered. What if the grandmother died after reconciling with her granddaughter but before she had time to change her will?*

NO CONTEST CLAUSE. If you have concerns that someone might challenge your will because they don't like what they receive or think your distribution is unfair, you might consider a "no contest" clause. This clause states that any person who challenges the will does not inherit anything. This clause can serve to discourage any disgruntled family member from challenging your will. Not all states uphold "no contest" clauses, so if the challenger loses they might still inherit what they were originally entitled.

➜ *SIDEBAR. Successful **challenges to a will** are difficult to do. To challenge a will a person must have "standing", meaning they are an heir, a spouse, a child, a creditor, or someone named in the will. They must also have some stake in the outcome. A challenger has the burden to prove the will is invalid. A will could be invalid if it was not signed or witnessed properly, if the signing was done under duress or fraud, or the decedent lacked testamentary capacity (meaning sound mind) at the time they made the will. Note, if the decedent made a will when they had testamentary capacity but later developed dementia or Alzheimer's disease, the will is still valid.*

SIMULTANEOUS DEATH CLAUSE. This clause prohibits any beneficiary to inherit from you if they die within a specified time after your death (for example, 90 days within your date of death). If this occurs, your estate will go to the next beneficiary in line. This clause is for situations in which you and your beneficiary die in the same incident or shortly thereafter. It makes little sense for your estate to go through your probate only to be probated again in your deceased beneficiaries' estate to then go to your next in line beneficiary. State law may dictate the length of the simultaneous death clause.

To illustrate, you and your spouse have wills stating that your estate goes to each other and when you both are deceased, your estate goes to your children. You and your spouse are in a car accident together. You die instantly, but your spouse dies 75 days after you. The simultaneous death clause acts to "skip" giving your estate to your spouse (whose estate must go through probate) and gives the estate directly to your children. The simultaneous death clause speeds up the administration of your estate.

APPOINTMENT OF PERSONAL REPRESENTATIVE. In this section, you name who is responsible for handling your estate and carrying out the wishes of your will. It is important to name at least one, but preferably two, backup personal representatives.

Within this provision, you can allow reimbursement of expenses that your personal representative may incur in connection with their duties of handling your estate. You may also allow for fair and reasonable compensation for services rendered. Generally, your family member will do this for free, but if your personal representative is a friend they may want some fair compensation. If you do not have anyone who could act as your personal representative, you could name an accountant, attorney, bank or trust company to serve as your personal representative.

Also, you may give your personal representative the power to hire or appoint people to help with handling your estate. For example, suppose you live in New York but have a condo in Florida. Your personal representative, who lives in New York, will have to deal with each state's probate courts. This power allows your personal representative to hire an attorney in Florida to handle that state's probate.

> ➔ *SIDEBAR. In choosing a personal representative, look for the same characteristics of your financial power of attorney. A personal representative should be comfortable handling money, be organized, and be willing to stand up to family members who want to interfere with the distribution of your estate. The personal representative can work with an estate planning attorney to guide them through the probate process so they do not need to be a professional. Designate someone you trust to follow the instructions of your will.*

POWERS OF PERSONAL REPRESENTATIVE. In your will, you list the powers of your personal representative. These include: handling your estate, paying off your debts, selling or leasing property, settling claims against your estate, making or retaining investments, continuing operations of business interests and making appropriate distributions to beneficiaries.

You can also give your personal representative the power to hold funds for any beneficiary that may be incapacitated due to a physical or mental illness or infirmity. For example, a personal representative could handle the money for a beneficiary suffering from autism or Alzheimer's disease. However, if you know one of your beneficiaries is unable to handle money due to a physical or mental illness or disability, seek an attorney's advice on setting up a trust for them. I will explain trusts in the next chapter.

A final note about personal representatives: it goes without saying that the person must be someone you trust implicitly. However, they will be held to a fiduciary duty, meaning they must only act in the best interest of your estate. A personal representative who does not carry out your wishes or engages in self-dealing can be subject to lawsuits.

> **Guardian** – One you designate who is responsible for the care of your minor children

APPOINTMENT OF GUARDIAN. If you have children less 18 years old, you will name a guardian if something happened to both of their parents. A guardian will have legal custody and be responsible for the care your children until your children reach the age of 18. As with the personal representative, it is a good idea to have at least one backup.

A court will strongly consider your choice of guardian. However, a court must act in the best interest of the child. For example, suppose you named your brother to be a guardian for your child but you didn't know he later became involved with drugs. Family members could petition the court and provide evidence that you would not have made that choice if you had that information. It is a good idea, in addition to naming guardianship in the will, that you also write a separate letter explaining the reasons for your choice. Again, a court gives your explanation great weight.

The appointment of a guardian is a tough choice and one of the main reasons why a will does not get written. I will talk later about factors to consider when choosing a guardian for minor children.

CONTINGENT TRUSTS. This provision is where you can prohibit a beneficiary from inheriting a share of your estate if they are under the age of legal majority, an age you designate, or some other incapacity, such as an intellectual or physical disability.

If you have young children, have your personal representative hold their inheritance in a trust for the benefit of your children. The personal representative gives distributions for your beneficiary's comfort, health, support, maintenance, and education.

Once they reach the age of legal majority, or the age you specify, the trust terminates. Your beneficiaries could then take their share of the inheritance. Some parents delay the age of inheritance beyond the age of 21 to allow their children to become more mature and financially responsible. Alternatively, you can distribute their inheritance in stages. For example, you could specify that one-third of the inheritance will be granted at age 21, one-third of the inheritance will be granted at age 25, and the remainder of the inheritance will be granted at age 30.

It may be tempting for some parents to make inheritances contingent on some event or behavior. For example, a parent might like to have a child come into money after they attend college, but what is the parent's idea of college? A 4-year college? A 2-year degree? What if the child doesn't go to college because they invented something, possibly becoming the next Bill Gates, and they could benefit from startup capital? What if the child wants to go to culinary school? It is not a good idea to "rule beyond the grave" as your good intentions could have unintended detrimental consequences.

Instead, consider writing a letter of your intentions and wishes for your children. I had clients who wanted their children to attend Catholic schools. While this was a nice idea and in keeping with their values, it may have resulted in unintended consequences. I asked my clients, "What if the nearest Catholic school was over an hour away?" and "What if your children lived in an area where the local public school was much better than the Catholic school?" and "What if another school gave opportunities of interest to your child, such as a high school for the arts, that couldn't be provided by a Catholic school?"

Rather than put that restriction in their will, I advised them to write a letter to the guardians about their wishes for Catholic schooling. They expressed their values and how they wanted their kids brought up with those values. That letter provides guidance to the guardians to make education decisions in the best interests of the children. A letter from you, although not an enforceable document, is a powerful and meaningful way to communicate your wishes on how you want your children raised.

Other incapacities covered by contingent trusts could be a legal incapacity (e.g. the beneficiary is in jail), physical illness (e.g. the beneficiary is in a coma), or mental incapacity (e.g. autism, Alzheimer's disease, etc.). Contingent trusts allow the personal representative to provide for those beneficiaries for as long as those conditions exist. Once the legal incapacity no longer exists (e.g. beneficiary gets out of jail), the beneficiary can then handle the trust proceeds.

OTHER PROVISIONS. There are other provisions that you could include in your will. There are protective provisions such as a "Spendthrift Clause" and a "Disclaiming Interest Clause."

A **spendthrift clause** prohibits a beneficiary from assigning or pledging their interest in an inheritance. For example, a son buys a Porsche with the promise to the car dealer that his inheritance will cover the cost. In this case, the personal representative or trustee is not bound to pay the car dealer.

A **disclaiming interest** is a different type of clause that allows a beneficiary to disclaim an inheritance. An example of this is if you have two children, Alice and Ben. Alice is a struggling artist. Ben is a Silicon Valley millionaire. Ben can disclaim his inheritance, which he clearly doesn't need, and his share can go to other beneficiaries.

You can also have a **mortgage provision.** If you are leaving a property to a beneficiary, a mortgage provision states that the beneficiary takes that property, mortgage and all. Therefore, your estate is not required to pay off any mortgage on the property. So, if you leave your daughter your house with a value of $300,000, but it has a $100,000 mortgage, your estate does not have to pay off the $100,000 which would reduce your estate.

A qualified estate planning attorney will also include other provisions to protect your interests as well as making sure your will is properly signed with the necessary witnesses. Laws vary from state to state on the proper requirements to make a will valid.

CHOOSING A GUARDIAN FOR MINOR CHILDREN

When making their wills, the biggest hurdle parents face is deciding who will care for their minor children.

Recognize that no one will be as good as you in understanding your children. However, that doesn't mean your guardian can't do their best. You must identify the next best person. It is not an easy decision, but one that you must make.

If you don't make this choice, you are leaving it up to a busy court who does not know your children or their potential guardians like you do! As one of my clients, with five children under the age of 18, told me: "I have to name someone as guardian because I am afraid no one will come forward to claim them!"

In making this important but vital decision, you may be facing one or more of these situations:

HESITATION. You have the perfect choice for your child's guardian, but you have not gotten around to naming them in a will yet. It is wonderful to have someone in mind. But consider the consequences if that person is not named the guardian in your will. They will have to petition a court and most probably hire and pay for a lawyer of their own to convince the court that they are the best choice. What if the court decides otherwise? Plus, who has the children during this period? What if other family members come into the picture? What if no one comes forward? Once you name someone as guardian in your will, the transition becomes easier for both the guardian and your children. Your other family members may have a better understanding and respect your wishes once they know you made the decision and put it down in writing. Consider that the cost of a will is significantly cheaper than a protracted guardianship battle in court.

RESERVATION. You have someone in mind who will be an excellent caregiver in raising your child, but they are horrible with money. Sometimes a wonderful guardian to your children may not be a great money manager. While it is optimal if your guardian can care for your children and handle your money, there are ways to safeguard both. In a will, you can name a guardian for your children <u>and</u> designate another person as "trustee" to handle the money in your estate. The trustee gives your guardian the money he or she needs for the health, support, maintenance, and education of your children.

> **Trustee** – One you designate who is responsible for the management, administration, and disbursements of any trusts created by you

CONFRONTATION. You and your spouse can't agree on who is the best guardian. Each of you has different people in mind for various reasons. This may not be as bad as it seems. You will need a guardian and a backup guardian if your first choice is unable to do it. Therefore, you can name both your choices of guardian, but you must determine who will be the primary guardian and who will be the backup guardian.

To select the best guardian, make a list of potential candidates with their strengths and weaknesses. Discuss the pros and cons of each of your candidates, such as their financial situation, their age and health, and their capacity to serve. Keep in mind that nobody is perfect.

In any of the above scenarios, have frank discussions with your candidates. Ask them tough questions about how they will raise your children. Will they follow your values and religious beliefs? Will they keep in close contact with other members of your extended family? Are they financially, physically, and emotionally capable of caring for your children? Such conversations may bring out a clear favorite you will both accept. An attorney can also be helpful in narrowing down your choices for the best fit.

Here are other considerations in choosing a guardian:

o How comfortable will your children be with your choice?

o Do they have a close relationship with the guardian?

o Is relocation involved or can they stay within their home area?

➔ **SIDEBAR.** *A letter from you to a personal representative, trustee or guardian can be persuasive. In addition to expressing your wishes about your child's future, it is helpful to include specific information about your child. Some information might include:*

- *Description of family life*
- *Education*
- *Medical care (doctors, dentists, medications, allergies)*
- *Special needs **
- *Behavior and management*
- *Description of interests and activities*
- *Religious or spiritual life*

* If you have children with special needs or disabilities, a description of their current abilities, needs for a full life, and the possibility of independent living provides helpful insight to those charged with their care.

CHANGES TO A WILL

As stated before, you may make changes to your will whenever you like. If it is a minor change, such as a change of personal representative or beneficiary, it can be done with a codicil. Although an attorney is entitled to charge for a codicil, it doesn't cost much. Be aware, however, an attorney who did not originally draft your will may not want to draft a codicil to your original will. By doing so, they are endorsing another attorney's work, which they may be reluctant to do. They would rather redraft your entire will because it will be their own work product with which they are familiar. Therefore, for a minor change to your will, it is most likely to be cheaper to go back to your original attorney.

Codicil – An amendment or change to your will

If you have a new will prepared, it will have language such as, *"I hereby revoke all prior wills and codicils previously made by me."* It is a good idea to destroy your old will to avoid it being confused with your new will. It is invalid anyway.

Do not make any notes on your original will! Handwritten changes or crossing out provisions to your will is not enforceable and may be considered in some jurisdictions as "revoking" your will. At best, the handwritten changes will cause confusion, litigation, and possibly unintended results. At worst, the changes or markings are considered a total rejection of your will and it will be revoked. A codicil has specific requirements to be enforceable with your will, such as requiring witnesses.

Some attorneys keep your original will on file for you. If this is the case, your family will contact the attorney once you pass. Other attorneys give you the original to keep in a safe place. If you have the original, keep it in a secure location such as a fireproof safe or safe deposit box. One caveat with a safe deposit box: once the bank is notified of your death, they may seal the safe deposit box, and your family will not have immediate access to it. The best place to keep a will is with your attorney or at your home.

→ **SIDEBAR.** *Review your will every 3-5 years and make any necessary adjustments. Ask the following questions:*

- *Are the guardians for your minor children alive?*
- *Are the guardians who you want?*
- *Is your personal representative alive and who you want?*
- *Are your beneficiaries alive and still who you want to inherit your estate?*
- *Would any of your dependents benefit from a Special Needs Trust?*
- *Is the disposition of your estate still in keeping with your wishes?*

One final note about making your will: Don't beat yourself up about not doing this sooner. Once you start the process, you will find a feeling of peace that comes with knowing you are protecting your family as best you can.

STEP 7

DETERMINE IF YOU NEED A TRUST

"While money can't buy happiness, it certainly lets you choose your own form of misery."
                                    – Groucho Marx

Now let's talk about trusts. This is usually the part where my clients' eyes glaze over. Trusts seem overly complicated and only applicable to the super-rich. However, there are several significant benefits to including a trust in your estate plan.

A trust is a tool to take assets out of your name (which would otherwise be held up in probate and may be subject to fees and taxation) and put it in the name of a trust. You retitle your personal property (real property and tangible and intangible property) into the name of the trust and the trust is the now the owner of the property.

Many people have the misconception that property or assets in a trust are not accessible. You can set up a trust where you are the beneficiary and draw money out for your care and support.

BENEFITS OF A TRUST

Setting up a trust has significant advantages. It will reduce the assets held in your name, thus reducing the value of your estate. The assets placed in the trust do not go through probate. Instead, the property in the trust benefits the trust beneficiaries you designate. There are other key benefits to a trust:

EASE OF ADMINISTRATION. With a trust, no probate administration is needed other than filing an administrative form along with the will. Your trustee handles your debts and your bequests in the same way a personal representative does. The trustee does not need to report to the probate court. This cuts down the time of estate administration to weeks, not months or years. Therefore, your heirs will be able to receive your assets and property without delay.

SIGNIFICANT SAVINGS ON ATTORNEY FEES AND PROBATE COSTS. Once you take assets out of your name, you reduce the size of your estate. Therefore, there is less to go through probate administration, saving you probate court fees. You will also save money on fees mandated by the state that a probate attorney may charge for representing your estate in probate court.

According to California Probate Code Section 10800, for an estate valued at $500,000, the statutory attorney fee is $13,000. In Florida, under Section 733.6171, the statutory attorney fee for a $500,000 estate is $15,000. These fees do not include any costs for the probate court itself or executor fees. Fees and costs vary from state to state.

AVOIDING PROBATE IN SEVERAL STATES. Your estate will have to file probate in any state that you own property. If you live in New York and own a condo in Florida, your personal representative will have to file two estate administrations, one in New York probate court and one Florida probate court. That means your estate will have to retain an attorney for each state and pay fees to each court. A trust avoids probate, so the property in your trust can be sold or distributed to your heirs without having to go through multiple probate administrations. So, in the above example, you would set up a revocable trust and transfer ownership of the Florida condo from your name to the name of the trust as the owner. This is done with a simple deed transfer. The trust would own the Florida condo. You will no longer have to go through probate in Florida.

PROTECTION IF YOU BECOME INCAPACITATED. If you become incapacitated and could no longer manage your affairs, your family will have to petition the court for a conservatorship. A conservatorship gives them legal authority to handle your affairs for your benefit.

> **Conservator** – A person appointed by a judge to manage the affairs of another who is incapacitated. A conservator of the estate manages the finances and a conservator of the person handles medical and personal decisions. The definitions and titles vary from state to state.

To get a conservatorship is a lengthy process and can be expensive. Your family will have to pay court costs, attorney fees and on-going fees for court supervision. The petition could be challenged by a family member who does not agree with the conservator.

With a trust, you have already designated the trustee(s) who will handle your affairs. They will not have to go to court and have a hearing on your capacity. Instead, the trustee needs one or more physicians to certify in writing that you are truly unable to manage your affairs before taking them over. The required number of physicians is defined in your trust document. During your incapacity, the trustee handles your estate for your benefit, and upon your death, the trustee will follow your instructions for the distribution of your trust property. Your trustees are held to a fiduciary standard as to act in your best interests.

PROTECTION FOR SPOUSE IN SECOND MARRIAGES. If you do not have a prenuptial agreement to address who receives your estate once you die, a trust could be set up to provide income to the surviving spouse yet control and preserve assets for the children of a previous marriage. There are many ways to address this, so it is best to consult an attorney for your particular situation.

EASIER ACCESS FOR YOUR MINOR CHILDREN. If you leave property or assets to a minor child, they cannot manage it. A court-appointed guardian will handle those assets and is obligated to make accounting reports to the court. If you have a trust, you designate who you want as the trustee of the trust. Your trustee manages the assets and provides them to the minor child for their care and necessary expenses.

KEEPING MONEY IN THE FAMILY. If you leave your child an inheritance and your child deposits it in their joint bank account with his or her spouse, it becomes joint property. While you may cherish your relationship with your daughter-in-law or son-in-law, you might feel differently if your child divorced them. Setting up a trust can benefit your child and your grandchildren so long as your child keeps those assets in the trust or separately in their name and designates your grandchildren as beneficiaries (not the spouse).

PROTECTION FOR YOUR CHILDREN. You may be concerned if you have a child who cannot manage money or has a drug or alcohol problem. If you leave your child an inheritance, they can spend it on anything they want, and what they inherit can be subject to their creditors' claims. If you set up a trust to benefit your child, your trustee will manage the money for the benefit of your child. You can make sure the money will help your child without being squandered.

> → *SIDEBAR. If you have a child or dependent with special needs, they may currently receive disability payments from the government. There is a way to provide for them after your death without jeopardizing what they receive in entitlements. A **Special Needs Trust** allows you to leave property to the trust for their benefit. They do not own, nor can they control the trust property. So instead of you leaving them property in your will, the Special Needs Trust is named as the beneficiary and holds that property for their benefit. You designate a trustee to manage the property and provide incidental support to your child or dependent under special rules to avoid endangering governmental assistance.*

PRIVACY. A trust keeps the details of your estate private. A will is recorded and made a public record in probate court. A trust rarely becomes public. If you don't want people to know what you have and who you are giving it to, consider a trust. Many celebrities and high-profile people set up trusts to keep their affairs private – you can too!

As you can see there are many benefits to adding a trust to your estate plan. Depending on the type of trust you set up, you are still able to use, benefit from, sell, or dispose of those assets as you normally would. Think of a trust as a corporation. A corporation holds assets in the corporate name, but it is for the benefit of the owners of the corporation. The owners of the corporation can buy and sell the assets and make all decisions about the assets, even though the assets are not in the owners' names. Once the corporation dissolves, the assets go to the owners or beneficiaries of the owners.

REVOCABLE TRUSTS

A **revocable trust** is also called a **living trust** which means you can cancel or revoke the trust at any time during your life. Once you die, your living trust becomes a **residuary trust**. You, as the initial trustee of your trust, have the power to manage the trust property, to add more assets to the trust, and to sell or dispose of assets in the trust. For example, if you put your primary residence in the trust, you can sell your home anytime. The proceeds of that sale remain trust property (therefore are protected from probate and estate taxes) but are available for your benefit.

WHAT GOES INTO
A REVOCABLE TRUST AGREEMENT

A revocable trust agreement will have certain provisions including the name of the trust grantor, the name of the initial trustee, a statement of property placed in the trust, and the names of the trust beneficiaries.

NAME OF GRANTOR OR TRUST CREATOR. You are the grantor, also called the creator, of the trust. Married couples might list both of their names as grantors if they are creating a joint or family trust. Alternatively, each spouse might create a trust in each of their names. This might work well for second marriages where assets are kept separately, or there are children from prior marriages and each parent wants to distribute their estate independently.

NAME OF INITIAL TRUSTEE. You will serve as the initial trustee of your trust. Married couples will list both their names as initial trustees if they have a joint or family trust. The trustee has the authority to manage the trust property, including the power to sell or dispose of the property in the trust. The trustee also follows the instructions outlined in the trust agreement.

NAME OF SUCCESSOR TRUSTEE(S). You designate others as successor trustees if you (and if you are married, your spouse) are incapacitated or deceased. Your successor trustee might be the same person you have selected as the personal representative in your will.

A STATEMENT OF PROPERTY PLACED IN THE TRUST. You acknowledge a writing, attached to the revocable trust agreement, which describes your property. On the attachment, you list your property to be placed in the trust.

NAME(S) OF TRUST BENEFICIARIES. You indicate who will benefit from the trust property and proceeds. Initially that might be you and your spouse, and then your children.

TRUST WITH POUR-OVER WILL

Even though a trust manages your property for your beneficiaries, it does not replace a will. A will is still necessary to designate guardians for your minor children. An attorney can prepare a trust agreement along with a "**pour-over will.**" A pour-over will instructs that any property not already in the trust will be transferred over to the trust, therefore "poured-over" into the trust. This is critical because most people do not get around to re-titling all their assets in the trust's name.

RETITLING ASSETS TO A TRUST

If you want the benefit of the trust, you must retitle your property in the name of the trust. You may need to open new bank accounts with the trust name and transfer money into those accounts. Or your bank may allow you to simply change the name on existing accounts. They may need to see your trust documents first. Remember, even though your name is not on the trust's bank account, if you are the trustee of the trust, you can write checks from that account. Retitling real estate into your trust can be done with a simple deed transfer, called a "quit claim" deed. If you have a mortgage on the real estate, you may need to get prior permission from the mortgage company to make the transfer to the trust. If your property is insured, notify the insurance company of the change in ownership. For other titled assets you own, you might retitle it to the trust as the trust owner, assign it to the trust, or have the trust as the beneficiary. An attorney can guide you to make sure all your property is properly transferred.

Although you may need to retitle some assets from your name to the name of your trust, the paperwork is minimal. You do not need a new EIN (entity identification number or tax identification number) for the trust nor do you have to file a separate tax return. Transactions on the assets of the trust are part of your personal tax return. So, for example, if you have interest accrued on investments in your trust, you declare that interest on your personal tax return. If you sold a real property in that trust, you declare the proceeds on your personal tax return.

IRREVOCABLE TRUSTS

Irrevocable trusts are different in that once the trust is executed, the trust can't be changed or canceled. Property transferred to your irrevocable trust is no longer considered part of your estate. Why would anyone want to set up an irrevocable trust if they can't change it? In short, to reduce one's estate and avoid paying state and/or federal estate taxes or to provide for spouses of second marriages.

In 2017, estates valued $5,490,000 or more had to file a federal estate tax return.[ix] With the new tax law enacted in December 2017, individual estates worth $11.2 million or married estates worth $22.4 million in 2018 will have to file a federal estate tax return. Federal estate tax laws can change at any time, so watch the headlines.

Some irrevocable trusts to consider are **QTIP Trusts, Charitable Remainder Trusts, Life Insurance Trusts,** and **Generation Skipping Trusts**. If you are thinking about any of these, I highly recommend consulting an attorney and an accountant as there are significant legal and tax rules and ramifications in setting up and maintaining these trusts.

QTIP TRUSTS

QTIP or **qualified terminable interest property trusts** can be used for second marriages. The trust is set up to let the surviving spouse use the trust property and receive income on the trust property of the decedent spouse for the remainder of the life of the surviving spouse. This is called a **"life estate."** Although the surviving spouse can benefit from the trust property, they cannot sell it or give it away. Once the surviving spouse dies, the trust property goes to the final beneficiaries, usually the decedent's heirs. Any tax liability on the decedent's estate is deferred until the death of the surviving spouse.

CHARITABLE TRUSTS

Charitable remainder trusts are where you make an irrevocable gift of property to a recognized tax-exempt charity. Once donated, this property is no longer an asset of your estate.

During your lifetime, you may receive income (either fixed or a percentage) on the trust property. When you die, the remainder of the property goes to the charity. For example, if you have a condo that you rent out, you continue to receive the monthly rent payments. Upon your death, the named charity will get the property. Alternatively, if you give the charity a sizeable monetary investment such as a bank account or stock, you can receive the interest or dividends. Upon your death, the money goes to the charity.

A charitable remainder trust is different than a **charitable lead trust** where you may designate income on a property to benefit a charity during your life. Upon your death, the property either goes to back to your estate or another charity. If you had a condo that you rent out, the monthly rent payments could go to the charity, but upon your death, the condo will be part of your estate to give to another named beneficiary. With an investment account or stock grant, the interest or dividends would benefit the charity during your life. Upon your death, your beneficiaries will receive the money.

LIFE INSURANCE TRUSTS

Life insurance trusts are where you transfer the ownership of your life insurance policies from you to the trust. Without a life insurance trust, upon your death, the proceeds of the policy are given tax-free to your beneficiaries but are calculated as part of your estate for federal estate tax purposes. If you have a life insurance trust, the proceeds are not part of your estate, which reduces the size of your estate. One caveat is that the trust must be set up three years prior to your death. Otherwise the proceeds will not be considered to have transferred from your estate and will be included in your taxable estate.

GENERATION SKIPPING TRUSTS

Generation skipping trusts are trusts set up for extremely wealthy families who want to give their children income only on the property but "skip" that generation to give the remaining property to their grandchildren. This type of trust is created to reduce the estates of the children who are so wealthy they do not want the inheritance to increase their estates. Any inheritance will "skip" them and go to the grandchildren.

> → **SIDEBAR.** *Most estate attorneys will tell you everyone needs a revocable trust. They are not wrong. However, if you are starting out with a little money and young kids, the critical document you need is a will to name guardians for your children. A trust is something you will want to have as you start to accumulate wealth or want to reduce the time and expense of probate as well as potential estate taxes.*
>
> *Do the math! A good rule of thumb is to estimate the value of your estate (calculate what property you own, the value of your house, bank accounts, stocks, bonds, other investments, etc.) and find out what estate taxes and probate fees your state may charge you. Probate fees alone may justify creating a revocable trust.*
>
> *If you own a home, an uptick in the housing market can quickly put your estate in a higher tax bracket. Look at comparable real estate values or consult a real estate agent to determine the value of your house. Your estate may be worth more than you think, especially if you live in an expensive real estate market!*
>
> *For example, in California, if you own a home worth $600,000 but have a $300,000 mortgage, estate taxes and fees are calculated on the $600,000 value (despite you only having $300,000 in equity).*

In summary, there are many advantages to setting up a trust. Consider the amount of time and expense it will take for an attorney to handle your probate. The cost of setting up and maintaining a trust will be significantly less than the probate costs, especially factoring in estate taxes.

The more you learn about trusts, the less scary and burdensome they will seem. You will understand how they can benefit you and your family.

STEP 8

PLAN FOR BUSINESS SALE OR SUCCESSION

"The biggest mistake a small business can make is to think like a small business."

– Anonymous

If you have created a business or currently run one, succession planning for that business is critical. The first question to ask is: "After my death, do I want this business to continue?" If it is a large business or a family-run business, the answer is probably yes. If so, start thinking about how to continue the business and who will run it. If the business is your own, primarily run by your expertise, then the plan might be to sell or close your business.

For example, if you have a service business such as baking elaborate cakes and you are the only one in your business, you probably have a little inventory and some equipment, but the expertise rests with your talents – not something transferable or saleable. However, if you have a business that makes a product, such as a medical device, you have inventory, equipment, some established sales channels, and your business could be sold or continued under other leadership.

You can plan for business succession in many ways. With a family-owned business, a transfer can be done by gift or with a "Buy and Sell Agreement." An attorney can draft agreements for an orderly transfer of responsibilities, and equitable distribution of assets and liabilities. The attorney will also address tax implications and resolve disputes among family members.

If business partners are not in the same family, the succession plan may be different. The first step is to determine the value of the business. It can be done by a certified public accountant's appraisal or by agreement of the partners or business owners. With the value of the business established, an attorney can draft agreements for a buyout of the deceased business partner. Some business owners use life insurance policies specifically for this purpose.

For example, a business owned by two partners is valued at $2 million by a certified public accountant. An attorney could draft an agreement whereby the business buys a $1 million life insurance policy on the life of each partner. Upon the death of one of the partners, the policy "buys" out the deceased partner's interest in the company. The $1 million from the death benefit goes to the deceased's family, and the remaining partner now has 100% interest in the company.

If you are looking to sell your company, get an independent valuation. Have your business attorney draft a "Buy and Sell Agreement." If you plan your business to conclude at your death, an attorney can help with the dissolution of the business. Alternatively, you could place instructions for the termination of your business within your last will and testament.

The important thing is to make sure you have a succession plan in place. Without a plan, you could put your business concern in jeopardy.

> → **SIDEBAR.** *If you have a business as a sole proprietorship, it is wise to have it incorporated to protect your personal assets from business liability. Forming a corporation, limited partnership, or limited liability company protects personal assets against claims or lawsuits made on your business. Consult with a business attorney on what is the best corporate structure for your situation.*

STEP 9

MEET WITH AN ESTATE PLANNING ATTORNEY

"He who represents himself has a fool for a client."
– Abraham Lincoln

Now that you have determined what steps you need to take with creating your estate plan, it is time to meet with an attorney. These days the practice of law is specialized, so it is a good idea to hire an estate planning attorney. Any lawyer can fill out form software. However, an estate planning attorney keeps abreast of significant changes in state and federal laws and taxes. They also understand the nuances of complex family situations. They are also the ones you consult to handle any changes to your will, for special situations that might crop up, or for probate matters.

HOW TO CHOOSE AN ATTORNEY

Choose a lawyer in a similar way of choosing a doctor. Word of mouth referrals are the best. Ask friends, family members, or coworkers if they have used an estate attorney and what was their experience. Ask for a referral from lawyers you know.

You can look for attorneys online through many lawyer directory websites such as Avvo (**www.avvo.com**) or Martindale Hubbell (**www.martindale.com**). You will be able to see information about them, any instances of professional misconduct, and reviews by client or peers. Find their law firm websites and learn more about their services and background.

WHAT TO EXPECT

When you make an appointment, most attorneys will send you a questionnaire to complete. They will ask basic information about your family, your family members, your assets, and any special needs such as having a child with a disability or other dependents. Some of the questions will include:

- Name and address of spouse

- Names, addresses and ages of children

- Your first and second choice of personal representatives and trustees

- Your first and second choice of guardians for minor children

- Your choice of beneficiaries and backup beneficiaries

- Your first and second choice of agent for Financial Power of Attorney

- Your first and second choice of agent for Healthcare Power of Attorney

- Addresses to real property, estimated value of property, and any mortgages

- List of bank and financial accounts and their balances

- List of retirement accounts, pensions, estimated value

- List of personal property (jewelry, cars, etc.)

- List of insurance policies and values

- List of any inheritances you might anticipate

Completing this before your consultation helps sort through some decisions you will be making. It also gives you a good idea of what property you own and the value, so you know what you are protecting and what you may be giving to your beneficiaries.

You do not need to bring in your taxes or list all your account numbers. Don't put off making an appointment because you don't have all the answers for your guardians, personal representatives, agents, trustees, etc. One of the many jobs your attorney has is to help guide you in making the right decisions by asking the right questions. I found those clients who were dead-locked or unsure about their designations (especially on the subject of guardians for their children) would come together on their decisions once I asked a few questions and posed several different scenarios that might apply to their situation.

The information you provide to your attorney is helpful for them to customize an estate plan for your specific situation.

When you meet with your attorney, he or she will go over the questionnaire and ask additional questions. At this meeting, the attorney outlines what documents they advise for you and gives you an estimate of what it will cost. Some attorneys charge a flat fee while others may bill on an hourly basis.

The attorney drafts your documents and sends them to you for your review. It is important to check the names and spelling of all your designated agents and beneficiaries. The attorney will have you sign your documents in the office with a notary and the required number of witnesses needed in your state. In many cases, an attorney keeps the originals and provides you with a set of copies.

Don't be afraid that you are "locked into it" once you sign your documents. If you want to any change any provisions, such as guardians or beneficiaries your attorney can draft a codicil.

In my practice, after our clients signed all their estate planning documents, there was usually an audible sigh of relief. These moments were the best part of my day. Many clients had put off estate planning for years (and even decades). It was nice to see our clients leave with a feeling of peace and the knowledge that they have organized their affairs for their family.

→ **SIDEBAR.** *Check with your employer to see if you have a **legal service plan** as an employee benefit. Legal service plans are where you pay a nominal fee from each paycheck to have access to a list of attorneys that provide basic legal services for free. Or you can subscribe to a prepaid legal service as an individual. Check online or with the American Bar Association (**www.americanbar.org**) for prepaid legal service plans. Most legal service plans have estate planning attorneys that can handle most, if not all, your estate planning needs.*

STEP 10

CREATE AN "IN CASE OF EMERGENCY" BINDER

"For every minute spent organizing, an hour is earned."
– Benjamin Franklin

When my Florida law practice drafted estate planning documents, we presented our clients with a **Legal & Financial Family Binder**. This binder was where they could put all their estate planning documents and essential financial information in one place. We called it the "911 Binder," meaning that when you got a call from the hospital, you could easily find the Health Care Power of Attorney. If you needed to go to a bank, you had the Financial Power of Attorney as well as a list of bank accounts and the key to a safety deposit box. In case of death, there is one place to find the will, organ donation information, and funeral arrangements. Because Florida is prone to hurricanes, people needing to evacuate quickly could find all their critical documents in one place (especially their homeowner's insurance policy)!

We thought this was helpful because in a crisis the last thing you need is to figure out where you put your documents! We also found it was great to have one place for families to share critical information. In many cases, one spouse handles most of the financial transactions, banking, insurance, etc., and the other spouse knows little, if any, of the finances. If the spouse with the financial knowledge dies, the other is overwhelmed with new information and responsibility. Having a binder can inform your family about what assets, accounts, policies and benefits they have.

There are many organizers and checklists online or available for purchase. However, you can easily customize a binder of your own. Organize your binder into sections such as family medical, financial, and legal information and put the details in the corresponding sections. For example, instead of filling out a form of who is your personal representative or executor of your will, beneficiaries of your will, etc., put a copy of the will in the binder and a note of where to find the original will. Instead of listing all your bank accounts and account numbers, put a copy of a recent statement in the binder. If you are more organized, you can draft a document on your computer with your essential information and update it when necessary. Keep an updated copy in the binder.

Your binder could have sections which include the following:

MY FAMILY INFORMATION

List all family members including parents, children, grandchildren with their names and contact information, dates of birth, marriage, and death. In case of emergency, it is one place to go for your updated contact information.

HEALTH CARE POWER OF ATTORNEY
& MEDICAL INFORMATION

Include your original Health Care Power of Attorney or a copy with instructions on where to find the original. If you have the original document, put it in a plastic sheet protector. Do not hole punch it or mark it up.

Include the names and contact information of your doctors and other medical professionals. Indicate what hospital or nursing facility you prefer. Detail your medical history, including any surgeries or procedures with their dates. List medications and supplements that you take. Include any specific allergies to food or medications. This section will be helpful for your Health Care Surrogate to provide your medical information to a new doctor.

HEALTH INSURANCE & MEDICAL BENEFITS

List your health insurance plans with group or plan numbers, contact information, and benefits. If you have government, military, or Long-Term Health Care benefits, disability insurance, or Medicare or Medicaid, list them are along with the contacts and phone numbers.

ADVANCE MEDICAL DIRECTIVE OR LIVING WILL

Include your original Advance Medical Directive or a copy with instructions on where to find the original. If you have the original document, put it in a plastic sheet protector. Do not hole punch it or mark it up. This section is where you can leave any detailed instructions on your end-of-life wishes or how your family can care for you.

FINANCIAL POWER OF ATTORNEY & FINANCIAL INFORMATION

Include your original Financial Power of Attorney or a copy with instructions on where to find the original. If you are including your original document, put it in a plastic sheet protector. Do not hole punch it or mark it up.

List all bank, savings, and investment accounts and the financial institutions where your accounts are held along with your account numbers. It is also helpful to provide names of those to contact at the bank. Keep a current or annual statement in the binder.

Include information on retirement accounts, pension plans, government or military benefits. List where the accounts are held and the account numbers. Put a copy of the retirement account or pension plan statements in the binder.

PROPERTY & ASSETS

List any real estate owned, cars, RVs, boats, etc. that you hold with copies of the deeds, titles, and information about the property. You might give instructions on what you want your beneficiary to do with the property you have given them in your will.

If you have a safe deposit box, list the bank location, safe deposit box number, and where to locate the safe deposit box key. Include a list of what might be found in your safe deposit box, such as certain documents, coins, jewelry, etc.

If you have a safe, leave instructions on where it can be found and who has access to it. List what will be found in the safe.

If you have a storage unit, include the address of the storage facility, unit number, where the key can be found, and what will be found in the unit.

> **→ SIDEBAR.** *Only you know best about what accounts, assets, and insurance policies you have. States receive millions of dollars of **"unclaimed property"** each year from forgotten CDs, bank accounts, pension plans, savings bonds, escrow accounts, insurance checks, security deposits, etc. If you have moved or changed jobs, it is possible that something may be left behind. You can search for unclaimed property in your name at the website **www.missingmoney.com** or your state's department of unclaimed property. Search in any state in which you have lived.*

BUSINESS INTERESTS & INFORMATION

If you have a business, list the corporate name, entity type, taxpayer identification number, etc. Include any contacts for the business such as a bookkeeper, CPA, or attorney. If you have stock certificates, you can put them in a plastic sleeve protector or attach a copy with instructions of where to find the originals. Give specific instructions about what to do with the business such as dissolve it, sell it or transfer it to another.

CREDIT CARD & DEBT INFORMATION

List your credit cards and any banks where you have loans. If you have signed a promissory note for a loan, include a copy of the note with the terms of the repayment. Include information on mortgages on your real estate, car loans, student loans, or personal lines of credit.

DIGITAL ASSETS & PASSWORDS

List passwords to bank account information and financial websites. This list is particularly helpful when one spouse may only have access to a specific site. Include information on all your social media accounts.

PROPERTY INSURANCE & OTHER INSURANCE

Include information with policy numbers and contacts on homeowner's insurance, renter's insurance, and car insurance. This section is particularly handy if you have to evacuate your home quickly due to a natural disaster or emergency. List details of any other coverage such as an umbrella policy.

LIFE INSURANCE POLICIES

If your family does not know what policies you have, they cannot collect them upon your passing. Insurance companies are not obligated to contact you about a life insurance policy they are holding, even if they learn that the insured has died. List where the policies are, with what company, and the expected benefit amounts. Attaching the policies is extremely helpful as the burden of contacting the insurance company upon your death is left up to the beneficiaries.

➔ *SIDEBAR. You can find out if a deceased family member had a life insurance policy. The National Association of Insurance Commissioners (NAIC) has a **life insurance policy locator** at the website **https://eapps.naic.org/life-policy-locator/#/welcome.***

WILL

Include your original will or a copy of your will with instructions on where to find the original. If you have your original will, put it in a plastic sheet protector. Do not hole punch it or mark it up as that may be considered a revocation of the will. Include any letters of instruction to your will such as your reasons for naming particular guardians for your children.

TRUST

Include your original trust or a copy of your trust with instructions on where to find the original. If you have your original trust document, put it in a plastic sheet protector. Do not hole punch it or mark it up. Include any letters of instruction to go along with your trust.

FUNERAL ARRANGEMENTS & ORGAN DONATION

List any special instructions or requests such as organ donation or cremation. If you have a funeral plan, include the contact name at the funeral home.

LETTER OF INSTRUCTION

If you have assembled all the above, congratulations! You have done more than 99.9% of people organizing their affairs. Another help to your family is to write a letter of instruction, your wishes, or items or issues not covered in your will.

For example, say you have a mortgage on your primary residence and on a small investment property and you plan to leave both properties to your spouse. You might let your spouse know you think it is advisable to sell the investment property to pay off the mortgage of the primary residence so your spouse does not have to worry about mortgage payments. This is not a provision you want in your will because circumstances could certainly change. However, it is helpful to provide suggestions that heirs could follow (if it made sense to do so at the time).

You can also write a letter to your family expressing your thoughts about your life and your death. Pass on any wisdom or words of comfort to those you leave behind.

Once you have your binder set up, review it at least once a year. If you are the person in your family who handles most, if not all, of the finances, it is a good idea to sit down with your spouse and go over the information with them. If you don't have a spouse, share your binder with a trusted family member or friend, such as your Financial Power of Attorney or personal representative.

➔ *SIDEBAR. A husband and wife I know have been married for over 40 years. Throughout the marriage the husband had managed all of the family finances. The wife never wanted much to do with it and was content to have him handle it all. Every year, before Christmas, he gives her a "gift" which is an envelope containing a list of all their financial accounts, what assets they have, etc. This way, the husband knows his wife has the necessary information if he should die before her.*

Keep your binder in a safe place such as a locked waterproof and fireproof cabinet or safe. Let someone know where to find your emergency binder and how to access it if you are incapacitated or unable to get it yourself.

➔ *SIDEBAR. Some people prefer forms and templates to help them get organized. If you are looking for forms to get you started on your **Family Binder** go to* My Family Binder Forms *at* **www.HodderInk.com** *for downloadable PDF Forms.*

PART

TWO

5 TALKS TO HAVE WITH YOUR PARENTS

Now that you have got your plans in order, are you ready to help your parents? When working with families in my practice, it was evident that most children want to do what is right for their parents. Yet many times there are disagreements among family members about what that might be.

Having open and frank discussions with your parents help avoid the stress and uncertainty about the future. It is a good idea to talk to parents about their wishes now instead of when they become much older or infirm. These talks will help them plan for future life events, resolve any conflicts within the family, and take the decision-making burden off of you.

There are five conversations to have with your parents:

→   The Financial Talk
→   The Health Care Talk
→   The Aging Talk
→   The End-of-Life Talk
→   The Family Legacy Talk

Before you start these talks, keep in mind the following to make the conversations easier and more productive.

TIPS FOR FAMILY DISCUSSIONS

BE PATIENT

Talking with your parents about their future will not be a one-time conversation but an on-going process. You must be patient and willing to wait until your parents feel comfortable. They will need to be "ready" to talk with you or to make certain decisions about their future. The hardest part will be for them to admit they need help and that you will be taking on more responsibility for them. Understand they still see you as their child who they should be helping, not the other way around. Try to feel out the right times to talk about healthcare concerns and when to talk about finances. Depending on your parents' personalities, one may be an easier conversation than the other.

BE TRANSPARENT WITH OTHER FAMILY MEMBERS

While it is tempting to manage all information about your parents and keep it to yourself, you may be perceived by other siblings as too secretive, controlling, or influential. Try to include siblings in conversations or at least give them updates on what is transpiring so there are no unpleasant surprises.

Most siblings will be happy for you to handle things as long as you keep them in the loop. Difficult siblings who have contrary opinions can be extremely challenging. But if you give them consistent updates, you can take some of the drama away from them. They can't accuse you of hiding something or going behind their back on some matter. Of course, if you have exceptionally difficult family members, realize that you can't please everyone all of the time, and focus on what is in the best interests of your parents.

KEEP NOTES

Since this is an ongoing process, when your parent expresses what they would like to do in the future, be ready to record their thoughts. Recording thoughts and wishes makes it easier to follow up in future conversations. Based on what they say, you can figure out what needs to be done and what steps to take. It is also helpful to have notes when updating siblings and family members. Your notes can also prompt future discussions. For example, you could say, "Mom, we talked about who gets your jewelry and china, but you haven't told us what you want to do with the house."

Keep in mind, however, that any notes or recordings regarding beneficiaries or giving away assets are not enforceable unless they are made part of their wills.

For example, if your parents' wills state that all jewelry shall go to their only daughter but their visiting daughter-in-law records that they want to give a diamond bracelet to her. In this instance, that recording is not an enforceable document and a probate court will not honor it. Your parents, if they genuinely want their daughter-in-law to have the bracelet, will have to make a change to their will or update their memorandum of specific bequests.

DON'T PRESSURE

Talking to your parents gently and without reproach will have better results than being confrontational. This is not a time to make things fair among siblings or to right past transgressions (real or perceived) within the family. The goal is to have your parents set out plans for their financial and medical future. You may not agree with how they may handle distributions, but their plan is better than no plan at all.

EMPATHIZE

Put yourself in your parents' shoes. How would that make you feel? Would you be scared of the future? How would you feel if you were losing control of your body and your mind? Would you want to talk about death? What if you could no longer work or enjoy social events and activities you once did?

Recognize that your aging parents may not want to focus on death. Discuss their thoughts and plans for the future without mentioning "death" or "dying." Use terms like "passing" or "no longer with us."

LISTEN

Sometimes the most important thing you can do to help someone is to just **listen without judgement**. A parent may need to express anger and anxiety over these preparations. There may be some bitterness at discovering their life did not turn out the way they wanted it. They may make accusations or blame themselves or their spouse for not taking responsibility sooner. Let your parents vent their frustrations and then help them work towards some resolutions.

CONSULT AN ATTORNEY

Making decisions to cover future life events is hard. Not only is an attorney skilled in making sure all the documents are correct and enforceable, but also a qualified estate attorney can raise questions you never contemplated. Everyone's family and circumstances are unique. Boilerplate or online forms cannot account for the particular needs of your family.

TALK 1

THE FINANCIAL TALK

*"The other night I ate at a real nice family restaurant.
Every table had an argument going."*
– George Carlin

Talking with your parents about money and finances may be more uncomfortable than talking to them about sex. They might feel defensive about mistakes they made or any debts they owe. Conversely, they may feel intensely private about what they have, fearing money-grubbing children will feel less inclined to be successful on their own or start asking them for money.

Emotions may run high when discussing personal finances. Try to plan a setting where they feel most comfortable and have only your direct family members involved. They may love your spouse like a son or daughter, but they might not feel comfortable discussing their money in their presence.

If they have a trusted banker, financial planner or account-ant, see if you can all attend a meeting together to discuss your parent's financial future. Get permission from your parents to speak with them.

Point out to your parents that if they don't keep track of their accounts, assets, life insurance policies, etc., their assets and money could be lost. If you don't know the life insurance policies they have, those beneficiaries can't collect on the policies, and the insurance company keeps their money. If you are not aware of all the bank accounts or assets they have, it may become unclaimed or abandoned property that eventually goes to the state. Your parents worked hard and saved for what they have. They won't want their money to go outside of their family. You may even consider starting them on an "In Case of Emergency" binder of their own.

Steer the conversation towards what estate planning they may need to do. Since you now understand the basics of estate planning, you can tell them the decisions you made and prompt them to form plans of their own.

Here are some conversation starters to get your parents talking about money:

CONVERSATION STARTERS

➢ "My spouse and I aren't rich. When we did our wills, we discovered that if we didn't make certain decisions, what little we have will be eaten up by taxes and probate fees."

➢ "I was going over my finances and realized my wife didn't know I had a small insurance policy from a former employer. If I hadn't told her about it, she or my family wouldn't know to collect on it if something happened to me."

➢ "Since I handle all the bills in my house, I realized that if I was hospitalized for some time, my bills or quarterly taxes won't be paid."

> "I put together a binder with all our legal and financial documents so my spouse has it. Now if something happens to either of us, we have one place to go for those documents."

> "I made a durable power of attorney so my spouse can handle certain transactions when I am away on business."

> "I reviewed my bank accounts and discovered that the bank had my ex-spouse still listed as the designated beneficiary."

Another idea might be to seek their advice and input. Parents love to give advice. If you ask them certain questions, you might get them to disclose their own financial decisions and plans.

> "I've been getting quotes on term and whole life insurance for my family, but I don't know how much to get. Do you have any life insurance policies?"

> "I was deciding whether to ask my brother to act as my personal representative if my spouse couldn't do it. How did you decide who to name as your personal representative?"

> "I've been considering a long-term health care insurance policy for me and my spouse. Do you think it is a good idea? Do you have one?"

Once you have a conversation going, you could ask them the following questions:

QUESTIONS TO ASK

- Where do you bank? What accounts do you have?

- What sources of income do you collect or anticipate?

- What expenses do you have or anticipate?

- What are your most significant expenses (i.e., mortgage, car payments, medical expenses, life insurance payments, etc.?

- Does your income meet your needs?

- Do you collect Social Security?

- Do you have significant debts? What is your plan for paying those debts?

- Do you own your home, or do you have a mortgage? What is the balance due?

- Who is your accountant, tax accountant, or CPA?

- Do you have to make quarterly federal or state tax payments?

- Do you have a safe or safe deposit box? Where is the key? Who has access?

- Who is your attorney?

- Do you have a Financial Power of Attorney? Who is it? Who is your backup?

- Where is your Financial Power of Attorney document?

o   Do you have a business or business interests?

o   If so, do you want the business sold or is there a succession plan in place?

o   Do you have a will? Where is the original? Who is the personal representative?

o   Do you have a trust? Where is the original? Who are the trustees?

o   Do you know how you want your estate distributed?

o   Do you need to provide for any dependents?

o   How do you want us to care for your pets?

o   Do you want to give to charity?

If your parents have difficulty with their finances, you could find resources for them, such as financial planners or debt counselors. If they are disorganized or forgetful, you could set them up with automatic deposits and automatic bill pay services. There are also many computer software programs like Quicken or online services such as Mint that help track finances and pay bills.

Once your parents are receptive about organizing their financial affairs you might inquire:

o   Can they consolidate credit card debt?

o   Can they cut down on the credit cards they need?

o   Do they have many accounts at different banks?

- o Could they switch all their banking to one bank or financial institution?

- o Can they rollover their IRA and other retirement accounts into one?

- o Can they organize their most important documents in one place (i.e., marriage certificate, military service records, passports, etc.)?

- o Can they set up online banking or automatic payments for monthly bills?

- o Can they set up overdraft protection on their bank account?

If your parents want to use only one bank or financial institution for convenience, be mindful of FDIC insurance limits. FDIC insurance covers deposits made in a bank or financial institution in the event the bank or financial institution fails. There are limits on the insurance coverage. The standard is $250,000 per depositor, per FDIC insured bank or financial institution. Check **www.fdic.gov** for updated rules and coverage.

You know your parents best, so you will know the right time and place to initiate small conversations to get them willing to share information with you.

➔ **SIDEBAR.** *Unfortunately, seniors are often the target of* **scams.** *Here are some tips to help protect your parents from being victims of fraud.*

- *Register their telephone numbers (both home and mobile phones) with the National Do Not Call Registry at* **www.donotcall.gov**. *You can opt out of unwanted telemarking calls or fraudulent solicitations. Tell your parents only to share their personal information with trusted people.*

- *Check the privacy settings on their mobile phones and help them set up memorable passwords to protect their information.*

- *If you have a Durable Power of Attorney, or if your parents let you, review their credit card and bank account statements for fraudulent or unwanted charges.*

- *Monitor people who have frequent, direct access to your parents. Find out who has a key to their house. Make sure any caregivers have proper background checks. Verify the credentials of financial planners or advisors.*

- *Invest in a shredder. Encourage your parents to shred junk mail, old bank statements or checks receipts with their credit card numbers, and any documents that they don't need but show their social security number.*

- *Warn your parents about scams you are hearing about so they can avoid them. Tell them to never give out their social security number, account numbers, PIN numbers, or passwords to people on the phone.*

- *Check with your local Better Business Bureau to verify a business is legitimate. The website for the Better Business Bureau has a scam search feature you can access at* **www.bbb.org**.

TALK 2

THE HEALTH CARE TALK

"Some people care too much, I think it's called love."
– A.A. Milne

Talking with your parents about their health is also sensitive territory. Your parents may not want to burden you with their medical issues or feel it is none of your business. However, if there was an emergency, do you know which doctor to call? Can you help your parents with medical decisions if they aren't able to do it themselves?

Since your parents may see multiple doctors, find out about all the medications they take and check if there are any problems with taking them all together. With their permission, go through their medicine cabinet to toss old or expired medicines. You will be able to see what prescriptions and medicines they take and ask them about their health issues.

You might offer to go along to doctor appointments with your parent if you are concerned about a specific health issue or to be another set of ears. Often, it's hard to understand (and remember) all the information a doctor is saying. And if you are the patient, it is easy to become overwhelmed. Accompany your parent and ask questions they may forget to ask. Or have the doctor simplify when explaining something. Bring a notebook to take down notes, or after they give you paperwork, make a few notes on it to summarize the conversation while it is still fresh in your mind.

Keeping tabs on your parents' mental health is important as well. Depression is not uncommon among the elderly and those who have had a lifetime struggle with depression may be feeling worse. As they age, memory loss may become a factor which could be compounded by stress, lack of proper sleep or nutrition, or side effects caused by medications. If you detect memory issues or dementia, helping your parents get treatment early can help them and potentially slow down a progressive decline.

Here are some conversation starters to get your parents talking about their health:

CONVERSATION STARTERS

> My mother-in-law recently got the shingles vaccine shot. Has your doctor recommended that you get one?

> I noticed you aren't going out with your friends as much as you used to, are you feeling okay?

> I just organized my medicine cabinet and cleaned out expired medicines. Can I help you go through yours?

> I hear a lot of things in the news about Medicare and Medicaid. What medical benefits do you have?

> I notice you are asking me the same questions over and over again. I am a little worried that you are having trouble remembering things. Have you mentioned this to your doctor?

When talking to your parents about their health, especially regarding memory issues, **tread lightly!** They may be especially sensitive to the troubles they are experiencing and become defensive. You might gently say, "Mother, we spoke about this yesterday and today, do you not recall? Maybe we can mention this to the doctor at your next appointment just to make sure there is nothing wrong. It's probably nothing. But if it is something, catching it early is key, and we can take preventative measures."

However, once they start sharing, you may want to ask them the following questions:

QUESTIONS TO ASK

o   Who are your doctors and why do you see them?

o   What medications do you take?

o   Is there one doctor or pharmacy who knows all the medications you are taking to avoid negative interactions?

o   Do you have any problems taking medications? Are you experiencing any side effects?

o   Do you need help organizing medications?

o   Do you need help remembering to take medications?

o   Are you able to get to your doctor appointments?

o   Did you get a flu shot this year?

o   What allergies do you have?

o   Are you up to date on vaccines?

o   Are you having trouble sleeping?

o   Have you felt dizzy or notice you have problems with your balance?

o   Do you have difficulty remembering things?

o   Do you feel depressed?

o   Do you have a Healthcare Power of Attorney? Who is it? Who is the backup?

o   Do you have Medicare or Medicaid coverage?

o   Who is your health insurance carrier?

o   Do you understand all the healthcare benefits you have?

o   Do you need help filling out insurance paperwork or claims?

➜ **SIDEBAR**. *If one parent is not in good health or having potential issues with memory or dementia, it is critical that the "healthier" parent get a Health Care Power of Attorney so someone other than their spouse can make decisions. If they currently have a Health Care Power of Attorney naming the spouse, they should update their document to remove that spouse from the healthcare decisions. If a parent is single or widowed, they should name someone, such as an adult child, as their Health Care Power of Attorney. This is also why it is so important to designate a backup Health Care Surrogate in your Health Care Power of Attorney document.*

TALK 3

THE AGING TALK

"Be nice to your children. After all, they are going to choose your nursing home."
– Steven Wright

No matter how much you plan for your parent's aging, it will be a challenge. However, having frank discussions with your parents will help you navigate the many decisions that they need to make.

If you notice that your parents aren't getting around as well as they used to, if you see unexplained bruising, difficulty driving or walking, forgetfulness and changes in mood, or less care for personal hygiene and cleanliness, it is essential to get them the help they need.

If they are demonstrating a sudden change in behavior, try to identify the underlying cause. If your parents become belligerent or are easily angered, they could be suffering from depression or illness. Even a UTI (urinary tract infection) can cause disorientation and irritability. If they are refusing to bathe or change their dirty clothes, their senses may be diminished with age. Or they may be afraid of slipping in the shower or tub. Talking with your parents can give you the information to help them address the challenges of aging.

Help can come in many forms and evolve as the needs of your parents change. Initially, you could arrange for house cleaning, laundry, and lawn mowing services and then add assistance for meal planning, shopping, and preparation. Then you could see if they needed further help with errands and transportation to and from appointments.

A NOTE ABOUT DRIVING

This is probably the most difficult issue to face with your parent as it is a true loss of their freedom. Signs that your parent shouldn't be driving are if they frequently get lost, have scratches and dents on their car, ignore traffic signs and rules of the road, have limited mobility where they can't turn their heads or respond quickly, and have "near misses" with other cars or objects. Medical events, such as seizures or strokes, can also trigger a ban on driving.

Gently raise your concerns and enlist the help of other family members who recognize that your parent is having more difficulty. You may need to contact your parent's doctor with your concerns so they can address it with them. In some cases, a doctor will tell your parent their driving days are over (so you don't have to). The doctor may also have the ability to order them to take a driving simulation test, which will test them for reflexes, and will clear them to drive. This is usually done through the occupational therapy department at the hospital. If your parent is permitted to drive, there may be certain restrictions on their driving privileges such as driving only during the day or not far from home.

In extreme situations, you may need to take (or hide) the car keys. Or disable their car by removing the battery or spark plugs. While it will certainly cause friction with your parent, you might be saving their life and the lives of others.

However, with driving services such as Uber and Lyft, and the abundance of things you can now get delivered to your home, your parents may not lose total independence. It will take some time for them to adjust to their new situation.

AGING IN PLACE

With all the resources of home health care and adult day care, the current trend is to "age in place." That is, to stay in your residence and not move to an assisted living facility or nursing home. The Washington Post cites a National Aging in Place Council (NAIPC) study that "more than 90 percent of older adults would prefer to age in place rather than move to senior housing."[x]

If your parents live on their own, look for ways to help them. Introduce them to technology or assistive aids that could make their lives easier and safer.

Some examples include:

- o Smoke detectors and carbon monoxide detectors

- o Programmable thermostats

- o Security lighting and cameras for outside the home

- o Internet connected cameras for inside the home

○   Assistive devices such Amazon's Alexa or Google Home

○   Automatic lighting (either on timers or lighting that turns on when they walk in a room)

○   Shower seats and grab bars in the shower

"Aging in place" is fine if they can get the support they need and can manage activities of daily living. However, depending on your parent's circumstances, this may not be feasible. You may need to look at alternatives when your parents can't live on their own.

If your parents have problems with **activities of daily living,** then more help is needed. Activities of daily living include cooking; cleaning; dressing; bathing; going to the bathroom unassisted; being able to take medications; hearing the doorbell, telephone, smoke alarms; etc. There are a number of options for assistance, you just have to find the most appropriate ones for the moment.

HOME HEALTH CARE

Home health care might be the next step in which your parents could get help for specific medical conditions and therapies as well as assistance in activities of daily living, sorting and monitoring medications, bathing, dressing, and help with toileting. Home health care could be through an agency or by hiring private care.

The benefit of using an agency is that the agency is responsible for all the payroll and taxes for your caregiver. If you have a long-term care insurance, the insurance company may pay the bills directly. You also have backup if your caregiver is sick. An agency, who has many caregivers, could send a substitute if your caregiver is unavailable.

There are many home health care agencies out there. Be sure to ask them questions about their screening and background checks. Get a sense of how they match you up with an appropriate caregiver. Do you get a dedicated caregiver for your family, or do they switch around caregivers? What training do the caregivers have? Is it appropriate for the care you are requesting? For example, if you need someone to be skilled in changing a catheter, do they have the experience?

Some people prefer not to use an agency, but instead hire a home caregiver through a friend's recommendation. Typically, this is a less expensive option than using an agency, and your parents may be more comfortable with having a familiar person in their home. However, it does have some drawbacks. You will be responsible for paying the caregiver directly. If they are considered your employee, you may have to provide tax withholding and benefits.

If you hire independently, do a thorough background and criminal check on the caregiver. There are online services to help you with this. You will need permission from your caregiver first. Get references from their former clients' and talk to each one. Ask plenty of questions so you are comfortable with your choice.

Finally, you may not get reimbursed for the cost of a caregiver if you use private help. Insurance companies may only reimburse home health care costs from recognized or approved agencies.

> → **SIDEBAR.** *If you or your parents' employ a caregiver privately, have the caregiver sign an **Independent Contractor Agreement**. This document states that the caregiver is not your employee but an independent contractor. If he or she is considered your employee, you are responsible for withholding taxes on his or her payroll, and you may have to provide worker's compensation and other benefits. Additionally, check with your tax accountant about the requirements for providing 1099-Misc forms for non-employee compensation.*

Insurance companies recognize that it is cheaper to have people live independently at home than go into a nursing home or senior facility. Some costs of home health care may be covered by medical insurance, long-term care insurance, Medicaid, veteran or government benefits. Some states or local funded agencies may also provide resources. Do a little research, and you may be pleasantly surprised that you have some home health care benefits.

HELPING THE CAREGIVER

Sometimes there is little you can do for the parent with significant medical issues, but you can help the parent who is the primary caregiver. In a case like this, give specific offers of help. Avoid the expression, "Let me know if you need anything." While you may be motivated with the best of intentions, it puts the task on them to ask for a favor. They may not want to bother you, or they may be too overwhelmed to know exactly what would be helpful.

Consider suggesting specific tasks that you could handle.

➤ Do you need help sorting out daily medicines?

➤ Do you need any prescriptions or groceries picked up?

➤ Can I come over once a week to do laundry? Or pay bills? Or help tidy up?

➤ Can I bring dinner over on Tuesdays?

➤ Can I come over one day for a couple of hours so you can get out of the house on your own?

If you live far from your loved ones and can't be physically present to help, consider offering to pay for a cleaning service, lawn service, meal delivery, laundry service, home-health aide, etc.

CAREGIVER RESOURCES

Another way you can help the caregiver is to find solutions for the next situation that comes up. If you can identify a problem the caregiver is facing, research answers for them. There are many online resources and support that address common problems and solutions to resolve them:

AARP	www.aarp.org
Aging Care	www.agingcare.com
Care.com	www.care.com
CareGiving.com	www.caregiving.com
Caring	www.caring.com
Family Caregiver Alliance	www.caregiver.org
Leezas Care Connection	www.leezascareconnection.org
National Alliance for Caregiving	www.caregiving.org
National Family Caregivers Assn	www.caregiveraction.org
The Caregiver Space	www.thecaregiverspace.org

CAREGIVER SUPPORT GROUPS

Sometimes the people who are directly responsible for the care aren't really equipped or experienced to do so. For example, the business executive who worked for 40 years outside of the home is faced with having to care for his or her spouse. The caregiver might even have limitations or health issues of their own.

Caregiving is often hard and lonely. Find support groups for the caregivers. They might benefit from talking with others in similar situations to realize they aren't alone. Support groups can be found in your community by looking online or contacting AARP.

There are online support groups as well, which is helpful if the caregiver can't get to local meetings. Most of the links above have caregiving support groups and forums. You may find some other caregiving groups through Facebook as well.

ADULT DAY CARE

Another resource to consider is adult day care. This is especially helpful if one parent is the primary caregiver to the other parent, or if you are the primary caregiver but have other responsibilities such as a job, family, or both.

An adult day care facility provides recreational and therapeutic activities, meals, social interaction, and monitoring medications. It allows the primary caregiver a break or respite from the constant care of his or her loved one. You can bring the parent to the facility, but some facilities provide transportation as well. Many insurance plans provide coverage for adult day care.

LIVING WITH YOU

Even in the closest of families, in the best of circumstances, having a parent move in with your family can cause a significant strain. It is best to be honest about the impact of such an arrangement on you and your family. Talk with your family about the potential new living arrangement and ask how everyone feels about it. Discuss it with your spouse and children and your siblings as well. Ask yourself if you can realistically care for your parent by answering:

Do you have a job, spouse, children, or other family responsibilities that will compete with the care you can give? With all your responsibilities, you must be realistic about how much time you have available for caring for your parent.

Would your parent accept living with you? Some parents want their independence or own space. Just because you think it is a good idea, doesn't mean they will automatically agree.

Is there enough space? Can your home accommodate your parent? Do you need to make modifications to your home? You may have to install ramps, safety bars, and lift chairs to handle their abilities or have enough space to accommodate a wheelchair. Does your home have a separate room or addition where your parent can have their space? Privacy is essential for both you and them.

Do you know enough about the care needed to help your parent? You must have access to their medical information and their doctors to understand how to provide the best care.

What is your relationship with your parent? If you have a problematic history with your parent, it will most likely not improve with the stress of caring for them. You may resent them, or they may refuse your help. Be realistic about your family dynamic. In that situation, you might not be the best caregiver for your parent.

Do you have the temperament to be a caregiver? While you may have the best of intentions to care for your parent, you may not be suited to be their best caregiver. It is difficult to accept that you may not be able to handle the stress of caring for an elderly or infirm person, especially if they have dementia or Alzheimer's disease. Focus on what is the best solution for your parent. That may ultimately be placing them in an assisted living or nursing home.

What are the increased costs? Estimate what the costs could be in caring for your parent. According to a 2014 study by Caring.com, 46% of family caregivers spend more than $5,000 per year on caregiving expenses. Of that 46%, 30% spend more than $10,000.[xi]

What if the parent's health becomes much worse? As your parent's health declines, at some point, you might not able to handle the degree of medical care needed. You will need a "Plan B" whether that is an assisted living facility, nursing home, or hospice care.

If the decision is made to have your parent move in with you or your family move in with your parent, make an agreement that sets out guidelines. Such an agreement might address responsibilities and who pays for certain expenses. Work out an acceptable solution for your parent(s) or other family members to share the costs of the care and living expenses.

→ **SIDEBAR.** *Have a backup plan. If caring for your parent in your home is too much for you and your family to handle, have an alternative. While it may not be your parent's first choice to go to an assisted living or nursing facility, it may not be as bad as you think. I have a friend whose 85-year old grandmother resisted going into "an old age home." She lived alone, then with her daughter, but her medical needs required her to be in a nursing facility. She was angry and bitterly fought the move. But after three months of living in the facility, she made friends and enjoyed the social activities and the food. The next time I saw her grandmother, her health was much improved. She told me how much she loved it there. Quite the turnaround!*

ASSISTED LIVING AND NURSING HOMES

If living at home or living with you is not an alternative, then your parents may need to move to a retirement community, assisted living facility, or nursing home. The best scenario is when they choose their own senior living facility. There are many options for senior living. There are resort-like facilities and facilities that meet the needs of the progressive aging stages such as independent living, assisted living, and nursing homes with memory care facilities.

If you can, encourage your parents to check out local senior living options. Your parents will immediately get a sense of what they like and don't like. Convince them it is like picking out a college. They helped you with that decision, now you can help them. Make a fun day of it.

Check out the facility, take a tour, and try the food. See what activities and amenities the facility offers. Find out what recreational, cultural and enrichment programs they have. Observe how the residents are dressed. Do they look clean and well groomed? Do you detect any unpleasant odors? Do the residents seem engaged and happy? Are the caregivers professional and friendly?

When visiting assisted living and nursing homes, take notes of what you observe. Come prepared with questions.

QUESTIONS TO ASK
ASSISTED LIVING AND NURSING HOMES

o   Is the facility accredited by JCHAHO (Joint Commission of the Accreditation of Healthcare Organizations)? JCHAHO is a not-for-profit organization that inspects and certifies healthcare organizations.

o   If you rely on Medicare to help with expenses, is it a Medicare approved facility?

o   Is there on-site access to health care?

o   Do you have to use their doctors?

o   Is the facility located near medical facilities?

o Does the facility provide transportation to medical appointments, shopping excursions, or cultural activities?

o What are the monthly expenses and fees for the facility?

o Can the fees be offset by Long-Term Health Care Insurance, Medicare or Medicaid?

o Are there large upfront fees or contracts?

o Is there a waiting list?

o What happens when the parents become terminally ill? Can they stay there, or do they have to move to another facility?

o What are the policies about visiting hours, pets, smoking?

o If you have a parent with dementia, is there a dedicated wing or secure area to prevent wandering or injury?

Even if your parent is in favor of the idea of moving into such a facility, the transition may be difficult. Some people who enjoy their privacy may not appreciate the spirit of a larger communal facility. Other people have a hard time with a change of situation.

Recognize that the first few months may be the most challenging. Try to make their new surroundings familiar by bringing their favorite objects to have in their room. Visit them regularly and encourage their friends and family to visit as well. See if you can get your parent involved in the day to day activities of the facility. Send change of address cards so their friends can keep in touch. Some facilities host family dinners or special events that you can attend.

Send your parent care packages or something to brighten their day.

> ➔ **SIDEBAR.** *When my grandmother moved into a retirement home she was reluctant to make friends which was very uncharacteristic of her. I would stop by on different weeknights for dinner at the communal dining room. A visiting grandchild always sparks interest and residents would come up and talk to us. Pretty soon my grandmother had a full table of new friends.*

If you find your parent becoming depressed or withdrawn upon moving to a new place, consult with the management for suggestions on handling the transition. Some facilities have resident mentor programs to help with the adjustment.

> ➔ **SIDEBAR.** *If your parents do not have a lot of income or assets, they might qualify for Medicaid to cover nursing home expenses. Some who don't yet qualify for Medicaid can "spend down" their assets to meet Medicaid eligibility requirements. **Medicaid "spend down" accounts** are extremely technical and have many regulations, so it is best to consult with an experienced Medicaid planning attorney.*

HOSPICE

Hospice or palliative care provides tremendous support for a family dealing with a life-limiting or terminal illness. Most hospice organizations are made up of a team of physicians, nurses, counselors, social workers, hospice aides, and volunteers who work together providing services to a patient and his or her family. The team assesses the needs of the patient and family and provides them with care and comfort throughout the progression of the disease. That care and comfort may encompass physical, emotional, social, and spiritual needs. Hospice can also provide respite for the caregiver and bereavement support.

Once considered an option for those with six months or less to live, some hospice organizations have expanded their scope to include those diagnosed with a terminal disease or a life-limiting illness such as Alzheimer's or ALS. Typically, a doctor initiates a referral to a hospice organization, but you could contact local hospice groups to find out what they do and when their services would be appropriate.

The goal of hospice or palliative care is not to cure the illness but make the patient as comfortable as possible as the disease or terminal illness progresses. Hospice services are not limited to patients who choose to stay at home but also to those in a nursing home or hospital. Hospice can be non-profit or for profit. Although some hospice services are eligible regardless of ability to pay, they may be covered under Medicare, Medicaid, and most private insurers.

The discussions about aging in place, assisted living, or retirement homes could start from what your parents experienced when dealing with their parents (your grandparents). Reminisce about how other family members handled their decisions to get your parents to talk about their plans.

You might try some conversation starters to get your parents talking about aging and their future plans.

CONVERSATION STARTERS

➢ "My friend's mother just moved into a local assisted living facility. Is that something you might consider if you couldn't live at home?"

➢ "My friend recently hired a caregiver to help her mother. Is that something you might find helpful? What would you like the caregiver to do?

➢ "Grandma had to move out of her house once she couldn't handle the stairs. Your house has a lot of steps; what would you do if you couldn't manage them?"

Once you have an opening, be prepared with questions for them.

QUESTIONS TO ASK

o Do you have a long-term care insurance policy? Do you know what the benefits are? Can we look at it together?

o If you needed help in the home, do you prefer private home care or home care through an agency?

o If you couldn't live in your home, where do you want to go?

o Have you visited any retirement homes or assisted living facilities? What did you like/dislike about them?

BRICK WALL MOMENTS

When talking with your parents about aging issues and suggesting help for them you will most likely have many "**brick wall moments.**" This is when a reasonable suggestion or a suggestion made from a place of love is met with strenuous resistance, to put it mildly. Either the parent puts up a brick wall and won't entertain the idea or you will want to hit your head against a brick wall in frustration. Oftentimes, both are true.

You will be told you don't understand what they are going through. You will be told you can't imagine what they are dealing with, and you will hear a hundred reasons why your suggestion would not help. **Stay strong.** It will take a time for your parents to accept a new idea, admit they need help, and acknowledge that they are entering a new phase in which they can't do it all themselves. **Be patient.** In time, you will be able to get them the help they need. It just won't be on your schedule.

You may find that at certain stages, you will get more cooperation. For example, if your parent falls and is admitted to the hospital, you can most likely to get them to agree to have grab bars installed in the bathroom. If your parent has a heart attack, you might convince them it is now time to pay someone else to shovel snow or mow the lawn.

If they have trouble getting around or managing stairs they might consider moving to another living situation that is more appropriate for their needs. Be patient and look for opportunities to get your parents' cooperation.

TALK 4

THE END-OF-LIFE TALK

"Life is pleasant. Death is peaceful. It's the transition that's troublesome."
– Isaac Asimov

If you are lucky, and persistent in the face of resistance, you will be able to have a conversation with your parents about their end-of-life wishes. Knowing what they would like to happen to them can give you peace of mind. Some topics you will want to discuss: advance medical directives, organ donations, and funeral arrangements.

ADVANCE MEDICAL DIRECTIVES

As previously explained, an advance medical directive puts the decision making in your parents' hands. They control what measures to take, what comfort and care they receive, and what life-prolonging measures they want. You honor them by following their instructions.

I had a client who was a neurosurgeon. When going over his advance medical directives, he shared with me some horror stories from his ER when patients did not make these decisions. Families spent days and weeks agonizing and arguing over what to do. Meanwhile, his patients lingered on, brain dead but kept alive with life support machines, causing much grief and extraordinary medical expenses. He said he wished it was mandatory for all patients entering the ER to have an advance medical directive on file to spare their families pain, doubt, and heartache.

ORGAN DONATION

It is important to find out if your parents are organ donors. You can check their advance medical directive or driver's license for indication of organ donation. If this is something your parents are considering, there is plenty of information at **www.organdonor.gov.** If your family member dies outside of a hospital and they are an organ donor, contact the hospital immediately.

Asking your parents about past experiences of family members or even discussing today's headlines about end-of-life decisions will prompt them to think about what they prefer.

CONVERSATION STARTERS

➤ Did you read that story in the paper about a woman being kept on life support even though her family disagreed about what she would have wanted? If that situation happened to you, what do you want us to do?

➤ Do you remember that grandma had a DNR order? What were the circumstances that made her ask for the order?

➤ Your dad insisted on dying at home with hospice instead of the hospital. What was your experience with hospice?

➤ When your brother died, he donated his organs. Are you an organ donor?

QUESTIONS TO ASK

○ If you were facing a terminal illness, what measures do you want us to take? Would you want life support if you had no brain activity?

○ Do you have an advance medical directive (living will)? What does it say?

○ Do you have a Do Not Resuscitate (DNR) order? Where is it?

○ Are you an organ donor? What organs are you donating? Who has that information?

Especially if your parents have specific ideas or instructions, encourage them to make a living will or advance medical directive. These instructions will spare you and your other family members the stress and angst of making those decisions.

➔ **SIDEBAR.** *If your parent is in failing health and they have a DNR or advance medical directive, provide a copy of it to any hospital or healthcare facility where they might be admitted. If your parent lives at home or with you, keep a separate copy in a conspicuous place. In case of emergency, give it to the emergency medical technician (EMT). A **Vial of L.I.F.E.** (Lifesaving Information for Emergencies) is a container which stores DNR orders, advance medical directives, and information on doctors, medications, and allergies. You can keep the vial in the refrigerator with a decal attached to the refrigerator or front door directing an EMT where to find it. You can download free information forms from **www.vialoflife.com**.*

FUNERAL ARRANGEMENTS

Rather than somber occasions, funerals are becoming more of a celebration of one's life and legacy. Personalized services now incorporate the deceased's family photos, interests and hobbies, video presentations, favorite music, etc.

Cremation is becoming more popular and so too are "green" funerals and natural burials. **Green funerals** are held in outdoor settings. Embalming is done with environmentally friendly products, or some people request no embalming. A **natural burial** means it is done without embalming and uses biodegradable shrouds or caskets made of sustainable materials. Headstones are replaced by stones or natural markers.

People are becoming educated consumers when planning funerals. The more planning made will prevent families overspending out of grief or guilt. According to a 2010 National Funeral Directors Association survey, "The average cost of a funeral is roughly $6,560" **which does not include the cost of a cemetery and burial vault**...on average a traditional funeral with burial will cost around $10,000.[xii] Those costs can easily increase, especially since the range of casket prices can vary from $1,000 to over $10,000.

If you can get your parents' wishes on funeral arrangements ahead of time, you will reduce a large amount of emotional spending. When visiting funeral homes, you can make decisions about the type of funeral they would like but do not feel pressured to give funeral homes money in advance. Some people opt, not only to pre-plan a funeral but pre-pay as well, therefore locking in expenses. If considering pre-payment, be sure to read all the fine print first.

Again, calling on your parent's experiences in handling funerals of their parents and other family members, may prompt them into telling you what they would like their plans to be. Try some conversation starters to get them talking about funeral plans and arrangements.

CONVERSATION STARTERS

➢ Your dad had a small memorial service, but your mom had a large church service. Have you thought about what you would like?

➢ Grandma and grandpa are buried in the town where you grew up. Where do you want to be buried?

➢ I remember your sister asked to be cremated. Would you prefer cremation to burial?

Once your parents are focusing on preparations, here are some questions to ask:

QUESTIONS TO ASK

o Have you made any funeral arrangements? Where is that information?

o Is there a funeral home you would like us to use?

o Do you prefer a burial or cremation?

o Do you prefer to be embalmed?

o Do you want an open or closed casket?

- ○ Have you picked out a casket or urn?

- ○ Do you have special clothing you want to be buried in?

- ○ If choosing cremation, where do you want your ashes to go? Scattered at a specific location? Or in an urn? Who do you want to keep the urn? Do you want it in a mausoleum?

- ○ Do you want any specific religious ceremonies or traditions?

- ○ If you want a mass or memorial service, are there special readings, scriptures or poems you would like? Any particular music or hymns?

- ○ Do you want a wake, Shiva or memorial service?

- ○ Would you prefer contributions to charities in lieu of flowers?

- ○ If you served in the military, do you want a military service with honors? Are you eligible for any benefits to help with burial costs?

- ○ Who do you want as your pallbearers?

- ○ What would you like to have on a headstone?

- ○ Do you have a family plot or preferred burial site?

- ○ What do you want your obituary to say?

- ○ Who do you want us to notify about your death?

If your parents aren't comfortable talking about their mortality, don't press the issue. If they don't have firm ideas of what they would want, then they most likely trust you to take care of the arrangements.

However, if they are somewhat agreeable to having this conversation and can tell you what they want, don't let the opportunity pass to make plans. It will be the last thing you will want to be doing when a parent has just died.

TALK 5

THE FAMILY LEGACY TALK

"The life of the dead is placed in the memory of the living."
– Cicero

Talking with your parents about their future need not be all gloomy. These are opportunities to relive happy memories, learn new stories, and preserve family history.

Capture their life experiences and wisdom to pass along to future generations. Ask your parents about how they met, their first jobs, and the historical events that they lived through. Ask open-ended questions (not ones that they can answer with a "yes" or "no") to promote longer, more substantive answers. You may want to ask them about your family tree, your family medical history, family recipes, heirlooms, and special memories.

YOUR FAMILY TREE

Genealogy has become more popular today because there are many resources to help you find your roots. Current websites such as **FamilySearch.org**, **Ancestry.com**, and **Genealogy.com** help you research census records and immigration lists to track your family lineage. Begin by making your family tree of what you know and ask your parents to fill in as much as they can recollect. You can even get military records from the National Archives (**www.archives.gov**).

It might be a fun activity for your parents to trace their lineage or follow up on immigration records. There may be continuing education classes that can help them as well as a wealth of information online.

Use care, however, when giving personal information to any website. Make sure it is a reputable service with good security. Read the privacy policies and opt out of any information sharing to protect your privacy.

FAMILY MEDICAL HISTORY

Gathering medical history on family members can help you understand your own medical history and alert you to particular diseases or conditions that are common in your family. Ask your parents what medical issues and illnesses your grandparents and other relatives had or currently have.

There are many family medical history forms online to help you organize medical information in one place and allow you to share with your family members. Recording medical history for you and your future generations can be invaluable. To protect your privacy, you can download forms from the internet and fill them out on your own. A Health Care Power of Attorney and Medical History form can be found at **www.HodderInk.com** at the My Family Binder tab.

There are also DNA testing services to provide insight on your genetics and give you an idea if there are any variants for a condition that may be carried in your family. Again, investigate the security and privacy protection policies of these companies. You might not want to expose your DNA information if it is not kept private or threatened by computer hacking.

FAMILY RECIPES

Who wants to lose grandma's cookie recipe? Or the secret ingredients in mom's lasagna? Or dad's award-winning chili recipe? Your family's recipe for Thanksgiving stuffing is clearly the best. Capture those favorite meals to preserve memories of family gatherings. Pass them on to future generations.

Grab the weathered recipe cards and make a recipe box. Make photocopies of the recipes and put them in a binder. You could even set up a video camera during Thanksgiving or a family gathering and record how everyone makes all the favorite family dishes.

There are also online resources to help capture those treasured meals. The following sites make it easy to record and publish your family cookbooks:

Blurb	www.blurb.com/cookbooks
Heritage Cookbook	www.heritagecookbook.com
Shutterfly	www.shutterfly.com

FAMILY HEIRLOOMS

If your parents are currently downsizing it may be an excellent opportunity to claim items that they no longer need or want but are important to you. If they have a will, they may have already made certain decisions. It gets trickier if they don't have a will or don't have a plan to sort out their personal property.

To avoid infighting among siblings, talk to your parents about how they want their personal effects distributed. Get their thoughts about what they want to give to each child or how they imagine their heirlooms will be disbursed. What they may value may not necessarily be treasured by others. Similarly, an item that they don't regard as valuable may be the exact thing that is bitterly fought over.

Create a discussion with your family. Your parents might be surprised that a daughter doesn't want the family china because she doesn't enjoy formal entertaining, or she has her own china pattern. They might find out a child really wants a beloved Christmas ornament that they remember from their childhood. There also may be two or more children who want the same family ring or antique chair. Talk with siblings about what is most important to them.

From these discussions, your parents can develop a plan. For some families, the parents have each child make a list, ranking what is important to them, and if there are any conflicts, the parents make the decision. Alternatively, there can be a lottery system where each child takes turns choosing items. I even heard of one family who gave their kids each a different colored sticker to place on the bottom of the items they wanted.

It is also important to balance fairness. If a daughter gets the family ring, silver, and china, the parents give can give the son other items of similar value or money equal to the value of the items.

Of course, family dynamics can be complicated with some family members feeling more deserving or entitled than others. Children, over the age of 18, should realize that there is no right to inherit from their parents. Unequal distribution among adult beneficiaries may be unfair but is perfectly legal. If a child isn't a minor, a parent can do whatever they wish with their estate, including not leaving their child a dime. As we would tell our clients: "Inheritance is a privilege, not a right."

➜ **SIDEBAR.** *A client once told me that his father had left his estate to his three children in equal amounts. He did not leave a list of specific items to be given to anyone in particular, probably figuring since the siblings got along, they would settle it among themselves. For the most part, everyone was happy with the distribution, except for one item. A ladder. An ordinary, dented ladder, splattered with years of paint. This was the thing that was fought over as the children had a great sentimental attachment to something their handyman father used for decades. Now they share the ladder and trade it from household to household. I am sure the father in drafting his will could not have imagined his ladder would be a source of conflict!*

However, you might face an entirely different challenge if your parents want to keep everything, or in extreme situations, become hoarders. Parents, especially those who have lived through the Great Depression or wartime rations, are reluctant to part with anything. This may be a way for them to maintain control over their surroundings.

The clutter can become an issue if it endangers them (i.e., causing them to trip and fall) or you need to move them to another living situation with limited space. If you have real concerns about compulsive behavior or hoarding, it is best to consult a doctor or therapist about it.

If your parents must downsize in order to move to another place, such as an assisted living facility, nursing home, or with you, they may be reluctant in parting with their possessions. Try to be sensitive to their feelings. Think of creative ways they can pare down items and still enjoy some degree of control. For example, if your mother has a ceramic collection that she is not able to take with her, take photographs of her collection and make it into a photo book that she could keep.

PRESERVING MEMORIES

Your parents can provide a family legacy of their memories. Getting the stories and histories can give you a fascinating look at the times in which they lived and invaluable information about your family.

Pull out family albums and take the time to record names and dates before it is all forgotten. Organize family letters. Scan the photos and letters into a digital scanner to preserve on DVDs, USB drives, or on cloud-based storage. Transfer old home movies from VCR tapes to digital media.

Go through scrapbooks and ask questions of your parents; it may reveal information you never knew. Pull out awards, medals, or news articles and ask them to give you the back story. You could even videotape these conversations with your parents about their lives which could be passed on to future generations.

There is a new trend among the elderly which is organizing their home and identifying what they would like to pass on to their family. Called "dostadning," a Swedish word for "death cleaning," people sort through their possessions. They make sure their valuable items are preserved and get rid of things they no longer want or need.

> ➔ **SIDEBAR.** *A word about parental privacy and secrets. A trusted child might ask if there are any sensitive items that should be destroyed (i.e., love letters, nude photos, embarrassing first novel attempts) or computer files. Your parent could have a box labeled "Private - Don't Look" with instructions to destroy the box upon their death.*

You may be surprised that by sorting through personal items with your parents you can resurrect many happy memories. You may even find stories that would otherwise be lost such as how grandpa got a medal in the Army or how grandma once marched in a civil rights rally.

A FINAL NOTE ABOUT THE 5 TALKS

Getting around to having all five talks with your parents may be a challenge. Look for opportunities to prompt conversation or actions. Moving to a new living situation would be a great time to go through family heirlooms. An unfortunate accident might be a good time to talk about safety around the home and health issues. If you have siblings, divide and conquer where one sibling discusses health issues and another sibling discusses finances. Family meetings can be helpful to plan for the future.

You may find your parents resistant to talk about these issues. They may stall or divert the conversation. They may even refuse to speak to you. Do not be discouraged if you are met with resistance. Keep working little by little to help your parents form a plan.

WHAT TO DO IF YOUR PARENTS DON'T WANT TO TALK

If you are having trouble talking with your parents, don't give up! Here are **ten basic questions** you might want to focus on to get the information you need. You could also write them down in a letter and have them fill it out.

Dear Mom and Dad,

I love you and I am concerned about your future. I want to do the right things for you as you age, so I need your guidance. I want to ask you the following questions which will help me help you.

1. ***Do you have an updated list of bank accounts, stocks held, retirement accounts, pension plans and other assets?*** *Does someone have that list, a spouse or family member, in case of sudden incapacity or death?*

2. ***Do you have a Financial Power of Attorney?*** *Who is your agent? Where is the document?*

3. ***Do you have a Health Care Power of Attorney?*** *Who is your surrogate? Where is the document?*

4. ***Do you have an Advance Medical Directive (Living Will)?*** *Who is your agent? Where is the document? What life-prolonging measures do you want us to take?*

164 | *Estate Planning for the Sandwich Generation*

5.   **If you have a business concern or investment property, how do you want those investments handled?** *Who will continue the business? Do you want the investments to be sold? Is there a succession plan or other instructions in place? Who is your accountant?*

6.   **Do you have a will and/or trust?** *How do you want the assets of your estate distributed? Is your will and/or trust updated and in accordance with your wishes? Who is your attorney?*

7.   **Do you have specific items such as jewelry, a car, or art that you want to give to a particular person?** *Is this written down? Where is the document?*

8.   **Do you have a safe deposit box?** *If so, with what bank? Who is authorized to access it? Where can a key be located?*

9.   **Do you have life insurance policies?** *If so, who are the insurance companies, where are the policies, who are the beneficiaries, and what are the benefit amounts?*

10.   **Do you have any wishes regarding funeral arrangements?** *Burial? Cremation? Organ donation? If you served in the military, do you want military honors? Do you have any charities that you wish donations to be made in your honor?*

Another idea, if you are truly having difficulty in communicating with your parents, is to leave this book with them. You might highlight areas that are particularly of concern to you. This might prompt them to take a look, start a conversation, and make some plans.

WHAT TO DO IF YOU ARE SINGLE

Are you single? Then you have plenty of company! According to The Washington Post, "There are now 109 million American, 18 and older, who are divorced, widowed or have always been single. That's 45 percent of the adult population."[xiii]

You may be single but still in the "Sandwich Generation," caring for your children and aging parents. Or you may have parents and no kids or have kids but no living parents. If you are single, estate planning is especially crucial since you are responsible for everyone.

MAKE A WILL

If you don't have a will, then the probate court will follow "intestate" rules of distribution and you may not like the result. Under intestate rules, if you have children, they will inherit your estate. If you don't have children, your estate will go to your parents. If your parents predecease you, then your siblings become the beneficiaries.

But what if you want to provide for a life partner or friend? Or donate to charity? Making your will allows you to specify who will inherit your estate according to your terms. And, as stated before, if you have minor children, it is important to name guardians for them. If you have pets, you will want to make provisions for their care.

PLAN FOR INCAPACITY

If you are incapacitated, you don't have a default spouse to step in and make decisions for you. You will want to decide who is in charge of your medical care and who will manage your money. Without naming a health care power of attorney or financial power of attorney, a loved one will have to go to court to get a conservatorship or guardianship over you, which takes time and money.

CONSIDER A TRUST

I have already outlined the benefits of a trust. For a single person, a trust can be an important tool to handle your money if you are incapacitated or to protect your money for your children if you die.

If you are single, follow Steps 1 through 10 to make your complete estate plan.

WHAT TO DO IF YOU DIVORCE

Going through a divorce is tough. The last thing you will want to do after your divorce is sit down with yet another attorney to go through your estate plan. However, you have just experienced a significant life event. Address what changes need to be made to your estate plan to preserve your assets and protect your children.

UPDATE YOUR WILL

Most states treat divorce as if your ex-spouse predeceased you, so your estate would effectively go to your next named beneficiaries. However, depending on your jurisdiction, that may not be the case. Family law attorneys recommend redrafting your will and other estate planning documents following a divorce.

Like it or not, if you have children and something happened to you, your ex-spouse will become their guardian. However, you must name backup guardians in the event your ex-spouse predeceases you or a court determines that your spouse is not fit to become the guardian.

CONSIDER A TRUST FOR MINOR CHILDREN

If you feel your ex-spouse might not be at good at managing the assets you left your children, you may consider setting up a revocable trust for them, naming someone other than your ex-spouse as trustee. Your trustee would manage the assets for the benefit of your children. This may be a good idea especially if your ex-spouse is remarried and/or has other children. You will want to preserve your assets to benefit your children.

CHECK BENEFICIARY DESIGNATIONS & UPDATE PROPERTY TITLES

Remember, certain assets aren't passed by your will, such as insurance policies, transfer on death bank accounts, retirement accounts, and annuities. If you don't change the beneficiary name on these accounts, these might transfer to your ex-spouse. Check all your property titles, and beneficiary forms to make sure that your assets are going to the correct beneficiaries.

UPDATE POWER OF ATTORNEY DOCUMENTS

If you don't want your ex-spouse to be in charge of your financial and medical decisions if you are incapacitated, you must change your power of attorney documents. Update any financial power of attorney, health care power of attorney, and advance medical directives in which you have named your ex-spouse to act as your agent or make decisions for you. You may not want your "ex" to be in charge of your medical treatment, your money, or your life!

DOUBLE-CHECK YOUR PARENTS' ESTATE PLAN

While unlikely, make sure that your parents have not named your ex-spouse as a beneficiary in their wills or for any bank account or life insurance policy. Similarly, check that they have not named him or her, even as a backup, as their financial power of attorney, health care power of attorney or agent for their advance medical directives.

WHAT TO DO IF YOU REMARRY

A subsequent marriage will bring a new set of questions and concerns to your estate planning. How will you want to care for your new spouse but also provide for your children? How will your new spouse want to provide for you but also take care of his or her children from a previous relationship?

If you remarry later in life, you and your new spouse may be interested in keeping your finances separate and preserve your assets for your respective children.

An estate planning attorney will have many options for you to consider such as a prenuptial agreement, a life estate, a trust, and life insurance.

PRENUPTIAL AGREEMENT

A prenuptial or postnuptial agreement can address who will benefit from which assets. Discuss how you will provide for any children from either of you and for any children that you might have together. You will determine who inherits certain family heirlooms.

Within a prenuptial or postnuptial agreement, you may choose to waive the right to the **"elective share."** An elective share is an option provided by states so a spouse is not disinherited. Under "elective share," a spouse has the option to reject what has been left them in the deceased spouse's will and instead "elect" to inherit 1/3 of the deceased spouse's estate.

LIFE ESTATE

If you own your home, you may want to leave your home as a **"life estate"** for your spouse, meaning they can live in the home for the remainder of his or her life. Upon the death of your spouse, the home would revert to your children or other named beneficiaries for their benefit. It is a good idea to address who will be responsible for the costs and maintenance of the home.

TRUST

You could also set up a trust and direct who your assets would benefit. The trust could provide an income for your spouse during their lifetime. Upon his or her death, the trust could benefit your children or other named beneficiaries. This could protect your estate from over-spenders, creditors, subsequent marriages, and divorces.

LIFE INSURANCE

You could use multiple life insurance policies as a tool to provide money for your spouse and any children. If you give your spouse a life estate in a home or benefits from a trust, your children will have to wait to receive their inheritance until your spouse dies. With life insurance, your children have immediate access to the proceeds upon your death. You could set up an irrevocable life insurance trust, where the trust is the policy owner and the beneficiary. The advantage of a life insurance trust is that the proceeds are still available to your children but are not part of your taxable estate.

It bears repeating that addressing these issues regarding subsequent marriages are best done by an estate planning attorney. They have the experience to guide you to the solutions best suited for your situation.

WHAT TO DO IF YOU HAVE A DEATH IN THE FAMILY

It is a difficult time after the death of a loved one. You will be grieving as well as handling various administrative tasks. You will have to make final arrangements, go through probate, and settle your loved one's affairs. A typical "to do" list includes:

GET LEGAL PRONOUNCEMENT OF DEATH

If your parent dies in a hospital or medical facility, a doctor or nurse will pronounce the death. If your parent dies at home and has hospice, contact hospice and they will handle this for you. If, however, your parent dies at home and does not have hospice care, call 911. Emergency medical personnel will arrive. Although it may not be necessary, alert them about any Do Not Resuscitate Orders.

CONTACT FRIENDS AND FAMILY

Give notice to those who will want to come for a funeral or memorial service. You could maintain an email contact list. Keep in mind that people, especially seniors and close family members, may prefer a phone call rather than a mass email.

MAKE FUNERAL ARRANGEMENTS

Contact the funeral home and meet with them to go over the arrangements. If you have a pre-planned funeral, it will be an easier process. However, you will have to confirm all of the details and information that they have on file.

SUBMIT AN OBITUARY TO A NEWSPAPER

Give details of a funeral mass or memorial service and if there is an opportunity to pay respects. If the decedent would prefer contributions to a charity made in their name instead of flowers, include information on the charitable organization.

OBTAIN DEATH CERTIFICATES

You will need original death certificates to submit to life insurance companies, Department of Motor Vehicles, probate court, etc. A funeral home is helpful in calculating how many you will need and ordering them for you. Since there is a charge per death certificate, ask the companies you deal with if they can return the certificate. If you provide a self-addressed stamped envelope with a request for the certificate return, some companies will return the certificate once they have reviewed it and made a copy for their records.

CONTACT ESTATE ATTORNEY

It is ideal if you can use the same estate planning attorney who has drafted the will for the probate administration. They are the most familiar with the decedent's estate, their family, and their wishes. They will file the will in probate court and handle the probate process. If that attorney is not available, look for an attorney who is well-versed in probate administration.

> ➔ **SIDEBAR.** *Although great for Hollywood drama, rarely is there a formal "reading of the will." Instead, an estate attorney will guide the personal representative as to who must be contacted about the estate administration and bequests. For some reason, my clients seem terribly disappointed upon learning that their heirs won't be gathered around a wood-paneled library wondering what they are getting or if they are cut out of the will.*

SECURE MAIL AND SAFEGUARD PROPERTY

Avoid identity theft by securing their mail or having it forwarded to you. By receiving the decedent's mail, you can pay bills, get bank statements, find out what the decedent owes, and what is due to the decedent. Keep other property locked up or in a secure location until distribution. Retrieve keys from service staff and caregivers and update any access codes.

PAY BILLS AND REVIEW BANK STATEMENTS

By going through the bills and bank statements, you can determine what bills need to be paid, what accounts to close, and where certain assets are located. You may review benefit statements to find assets you might not have known about. Look for insurance premium bills, as they will alert you to potential insurance policies on which to collect. Once probate is opened, the personal representative opens up a checking account for the estate and handles paying the expenses.

ALERT SOCIAL SECURITY TO END BENEFITS

Contact the Social Security Administration at 800-772-1213 to report the death. The funeral director can also help with this. Determine if a surviving family member, such as a spouse, can collect death benefits, monthly benefits, or a larger Social Security benefit.

CANCEL CREDIT CARDS

Contact all credit card companies to close the decedent's accounts. This prevents reoccurring charges and fees and fraudulent charges or identity theft.

NOTIFY CREDIT REPORTING AGENCIES

Prevent identity theft by contacting the three credit scoring agencies and request that they flag the decedent's account as "Deceased. Do Not Issue Credit." The agencies are:

AGENCY	PHONE #	WEBSITE
Experian	888-397-3742	www.experian.com
Equifax	800-685-1111	www.equifax.com
Transunion	800-888-4213	www.transunion.com

CLOSE ONLINE AND SOCIAL MEDIA ACCOUNTS

To date, there is no federal legislation which governs digital assets or property of the deceased. Digital assets include websites, blogs, Facebook, Instagram, Twitter accounts, email accounts such as Google, Yahoo, etc. Some states have laws to protect those digital assets and allow the fiduciaries or personal representatives to manage those assets. Other states rely on the provider's terms of service or privacy policies as to who may have access to the decedent's account. Consult with your probate attorney about the specific laws in that state. With Facebook, you can delete the decedent's Facebook account or create a "Memorialized Account" where you can retitle the account will as "Remembering" and allows friends and family to leave comments, photos, and memories of the deceased.

CANCEL DRIVER'S LICENSE

Contact the Department of Motor Vehicles to have them clear the decedent's name from the DMV records to stop mailings and prevent fraud.

CONTACT LIFE INSURANCE COMPANIES

You will have to complete a form and send a death certificate to the insurance companies. Remember, they are not going to notify you to collect on the policy!

FILE TAX RETURNS

Depending on the size of the estate, certain tax forms must be filed. There is the Form 1040 for income of the last year of the taxpayer. Form 706, which is the federal estate tax return, is due within nine months of the decedent's passing. Consult your probate attorney and accountant as to what tax forms you must file for the estate.

➜ **SIDEBAR.** *Usually an obituary communicates when and where a funeral or burial is held. This is also an advertisement that family members will not be at home. Plan to have a friend or neighbor stay at home during the service to thwart any burglars.*

WHAT TO DO IF YOU HAVE TROUBLE MANAGING IT ALL

If you have gotten this far - congratulations!

You now know what to do to protect your kids and how to help your parents. You are familiar with the fundamentals of estate planning and know what documents you need to complete your planning. You may have taken many of these steps already.

But what about you?

Despite all the pressures and responsibilities of caring for your children and your parents, it is important to take care of yourself first.

You know the emergency instructions flight attendants give about putting on your oxygen mask before helping your children? It is true about caring for others. If you aren't healthy, you can't help anyone else. Caring for a loved one, especially one who has difficulties or has a serious illness, can take its toll emotionally and physically. Find outlets for your stress whether its exercise, meditation, date nights with your spouse, or getting together with friends.

Get support for yourself so you can help others.

Some suggestions:

SEEK HELP FROM A THERAPIST

A therapist can be an excellent resource for you to let out your worries, stress, and frustration about your situation. Sometimes talking to a neutral party can help you deal with the difficulties you face. A therapist can recommend coping strategies for your situation.

FIND CAREGIVER SUPPORT GROUPS

There are many support groups for caregivers and even for specific illnesses such as Alzheimer's disease or cancer. It can be helpful to hear about other caregivers' experiences and learn how they have solved problems. They may have dealt with the same issues you are dealing with, and they can tell you what to expect as a caregiver. Many online support groups and blogs provide sound advice, encouragement, and even a little humor, so you don't feel like you are alone in this.

GIVE YOURSELF A BREAK

While it may seem counterintuitive to take a break from caring for a loved one, you need to take regular breaks to keep mentally and physically healthy. Give yourself permission to recharge yourself. Schedule weekly or monthly massages. Have a standing date to walk with a friend. You may feel guilty, but investing in self-care can prevent burnout and make you a better caregiver.

SET BOUNDARIES

It is important not to lose yourself while caring for others. While that is easier said than done, carve out time for yourself.

Make rules of when you are "off-duty," such as a one day each week or after 6 pm each night. Having rules will force your family or yourself to find alternative help, so it does not always fall upon you if your parents need help during those times.

FIND RESPITE CARE

See who might be able to watch over your loved one while you take a mini-vacation. Home care agencies may be able to provide caregivers for a brief time allowing you to get a break. Some nursing homes or adult care centers can accommodate a patient for a bit. Hospice can also be helpful in finding you respite care.

ASK FOR HELP

It is hard to ask for help, especially if you are busy running from one task to the next. But look for ways you can delegate to others. Ask for specific help from those who offer. Can someone else handle meals, medications, laundry, taking someone to doctor appointments, etc.? As you go about your daily caregiving duties ask yourself if another couldn't do this particular task. Make a mental (or written) note on routine activities that could be handled by someone else. That way you can be prepared when people offer assistance.

EMBRACE THE CHAOS

Sometimes you have to give into the fact that life is going to be difficult. Caring for children and parents is hard, messy, stressful, and frustrating. I could go on. Accept that you may not have a clean house and eat take-out more than you'd like. Now is the time to let go of perfectionism. Or as my dad would say "Don't sweat the small stuff and pretty soon you will realize it is all small stuff."

LAUGH A LITTLE

Try to find humor in the little things. Toward the end of her life, my grandmother was hospitalized for three months. Despite juggling her time caring for her family and running a business, my mother always made time to check in on my grandmother. On one of her daily visits, my grandmother commented that my mother's skirt was a little too short. My mother was taken aback. She thought, with everything going on, this is what she is was concerned about? We had to laugh. As critically sick as my grandmother was, she couldn't stop being a mother to her child.

FORGIVE YOURSELF

Caregiving is not for the faint of heart. It takes great strength and responsibility to care for another. It also takes a huge emotional toll on you. No caregiver is perfect. You will get frustrated, lose your temper, mess things up, say things you regret, neglect other family members, wish things were different, and then you will feel guilty for all of the above. Forgive yourself when you have bad days and realize you are doing the best under the circumstances.

HAVE PERSPECTIVE

Recognize that this time of being "sandwiched" at both ends is temporary. Children grow up and parents unfortunately die. Don't try to do everything yourself. If you need to delegate more, spend more on cleaning services or take-out meals, remember that it is not going to last forever. Do the best you can with what you have.

"Tough times never last, but tough people do."
– Robert H. Schuller

AFTERWORD

Dear Reader,

Thank you for reading my book. Estate planning, although not an exciting topic, is one I am passionate about.

I hope you have learned some valuable tips and are now empowered complete your estate plans. I also hope you have new strategies for helping your parents as they age.

And finally, it is my wish that your "brick wall moments" will be few and far between.

All the best,

Catherine

P.S. If you found this book helpful, could you please take a minute and leave a review? I appreciate your support in spreading the word to others.

Looking for more tips for the Sandwich Generation? Visit **www.HodderInk.com** or connect with me on:

Facebook: sandgenlife
Twitter: sandgenlife
Instagram: sandgenlife
Pinterest: sandgenlife

ACKNOWLEDGMENTS

Editorial cartoonist, Frank Tyger, said, "If a person gives you his time he can give no more precious gift." This book could not have been written without many wonderful people who have gifted me their time. I would like to thank the following:

My early readers and cheerleaders of this book: Shari Schwartz, Joan McNamara, Kathy Storm, Andrea Doyle, Eileen Edmunds, Jennifer McCabe, Gina Shrestha, Tara Paparo, Janine Musholt, Subha Tholudur, Shellie Johnson, Saroj Patel, and Debbie McNulty. Thank you for your unwavering encouragement and enthusiasm. And thank you for sharing your stories of living in the Sandwich Generation.

Kevin O'Brien, Esq. who, by helping our family, unwittingly started my interest in estate planning law and Ginger Weiss, for her expertise in all insurance matters.

Estate planning attorneys: Elizabeth J. Ferguson, Esq., Hope Wood, Esq., Karrie Bunting, Esq., Kelly C. Sturmthal, and Michael Brennan, Esq. for their knowledge and sharp legal review.

Fellow authors and editors: Bridget Hodder, Laurel A. Wicks, Bobbi Carducci, and Robert Henry, whose edits and suggestions made this a better book.

And last, but certainly not least, I'd like to thank:

My husband, Peter, quite literally my "rock," who makes all my impossible dreams possible.

My sister, Laura, who without her humor and support, I would not be able to survive the Sandwich Generation, let alone write a book about it.

INDEX

ENDNOTES

i Parker, K. (2013, January 30). The Sandwich Generation: Rising Financial Burdens for Middle-Aged Americans. Retrieved from www.pewsocialtrends.org.

iihttps://www.consumerreports.org/cro/magazine/2012/09/legal-diy-websites-are-no-match-for-a-pro/index.htm.

iiihttp://www.oprah.com/omagazine/suze-ormans-twelve-steps-to-wealth-step-8.

iv Social Security Administration, SSA Publication No. 05-10029. (2015, May). Retrieved from www.socialsecurity.gov.

v https://eligibility.com/state-disability-insurance

vi http://www.nasi.org/learn/socialsecurity/retirement-age

vii *Disability Insurance: A Missing Piece in the Financial Security Puzzle* (Publication). (2004). America's Health Insurance Plans Society of Actuaries Disability Chart Book Task Force. Retrieved from http://www.actuarialfoundation.org/consumer/disability_chartbook.pdf.

viii DiUlio, N. (2018, March 12). More Than Half of American Adults Don't Have a Will, 2017 Survey Shows. Retrieved from https://www.caring.com/articles/wills-survey-2017.

ix What's New - Estate and Gift Tax. (2017, January 18). Retrieved from www.irs.gov/business/small-business-self-employed/whats-new-estate-and-gift-tax.

[x] Lerner, M. (2016, January 1). New Online Service Targets Aging-In-Place Residents. Retrieved from www.washingtonpost.com/news/where-we-live/wp/2016/01/19/new-online-service-targets-aging-in-place-residents.

[xi] Nearly Half of Family Caregivers Spend Over $5,000 Per Year on Caregiving Costs. (2014, September 15). Retrieved from www.caring.com/about/news-room/costs-of-caregiving-2014.

[xii] Ropchan, J. (2013, May 20). Average Cost of a Funeral in the United States. Retrieved from www.resources.yourtribute.com/funeral-planning/average-cost-of-a-funeral.

[xiii] DePaulo, B. (2016, September 20). What Has Changed For Single Americans In The Past Decade. Retrieved from www.washingtonpost.com/news/soloish/wp/2016/09/20/what-has-changed-for-single-americans-in-the-past-decade.

CPSIA information can be obtained
at www.ICGtesting.com
Printed in the USA
LVHW081449050120
642548LV00024B/3034/P